A Tower of Strength

Two Hundred years of the
Royal School for Deaf Children Margate

By the same author

The Big Ship – Brunel's Great Eastern (London 1969)
The Crystal Palace (London 1970)
A History of Lighthouses (London 1971)
A History of Tunnels (London 1972)
The Wipers Times (London 1973)
Victorian Parlour Games for Today (London 1974)
The Spice of Life (London 1979)

A TOWER OF STRENGTH

Two Hundred Years of the Royal School for Deaf Children Margate

Patrick Beaver

Foreword by
Jeffrey Archer

Introduction by
Jack Ashley, CH., PC.

The Book Guild Ltd.
Sussex, England

The Book Guild Ltd.
25 High Street,
Lewes, Sussex

First published 1992

Set in Baskerville
Typesetting by Kudos Graphics
Slinfold, West Sussex

Printed in Great Britain by
Antony Rowe Ltd.
Chippenham, Wiltshire.

A catalogue record for this book is available from the British Library

ISBN 0 86332 732 X

THE ROYAL SCHOOL
FOR DEAF CHILDREN MARGATE

The problems of deafness are deeper and more complex, if not more important than those of blindness. Deafness is a much worse misfortune, for it means the loss of the most vital stimulus – the sound of the voice – that brings language, sets thoughts astir and keeps us in the intellectual company of man.

Helen Keller

CONTENTS

LIST OF ILLUSTRATIONS

FOREWORD

Before schools like the Royal School for Deaf Children were established there were few ways a deaf person could learn to communicate with the world. Any teaching or help available tended to be only for those who could afford it. At that time deafness was generally interpreted as a kind of intellectual deficiency.

In 1792 The Royal School was founded as the first free school in England for the teaching of deaf children from poor families. This history spotlights the methods of deaf education over the years and the perilous ups and downs of administration, as well as painting portraits of some of the impassioned and dedicated teachers who devoted their lives to everything the school embodied.

Finely illustrated and well-researched, this book is a rewarding and moving story for all of us (whether deaf or not) since it describes an area of experience that is profoundly human and full of majesty – the majesty of people trying to overcome a huge disadvantage.

Jeffrey Archer

The author wishes to thank all those of the Royal School for Deaf Children who have helped him in compiling this history. He is particularly indebted to the school's Archivist, Keith Campany.

INTRODUCTION

The first professional teacher of the deaf in Britain was Henry Baker, in the 18th century. Like others he confined his efforts to the children of the wealthy and it was not until 1792, the year when Thomas Paine published the second part of his *Rights of Man*, that a free school was founded. This early school, forerunner of the Royal School, and situated in the East End of London was called the Asylum for the Deaf and Dumb.

At the time the school was founded the deaf were thought to be beyond help. The notion that 'without speech there can be no reason', was widely held. Fortunately, people such as Samuel Heinicke took note of the fact that deaf children cry, laugh and shout quite normally and from this judged that since the children had normal vocal abilities, they could be taught to use them.

Throughout its two hundred years, the Royal School has helped thousands of children communicate with a world that for a long time was 'deaf' to their needs. When the school was opened there were six children; since then 10,000 deaf children have attended the Royal School and today there are 165, mainly resident youngsters. Thanks to the work of the School, children have been enabled to break out of the silence and learn to unlock their potential.

This well-informed salute to the work that the School has done over the years is also a tribute to the indomitable spirit of deaf children everywhere who have struggled against their disability. An account that should be ready by everyone, it is as much a social history as a testimony to courage.

Jack Ashley CH., PC.

1

The Background

Though endowed with a passionate and lively temperament and ever fond of the distractions offered by society, I was soon obliged to seclude myself and live in solitude.

Beethoven

The Royal School for Deaf Children was founded in 1792 in London's East End as the Asylum for the Deaf and Dumb Children of the Poor. It was the first free school for deaf children in this country and only the third in the world. At first it educated and cared for six deaf pauper children in a house which was an 'Asylum' both in name and nature. During its two hundred years the school has seen nine reigns, seven major wars and any number of economic crises; and during that time it has grown steadily and unceasingly both in size and function. Almost from the beginning it led the way and has been at times synonymous with the development of deaf education. Charles Dickens was a governor of the school and in his short story, *Doctor Marigold*, written in 1865, he tells how the 'doctor' adopts Sophie, a poor deaf girl, and tries to teach her to read. Later in the story Sophie attends a school for the deaf which must be the Asylum for Deaf and Dumb Children.

At the time of the school's foundation there were only twelve schools for the deaf in the whole of Europe and, with the exception of one establishment founded in Paris in 1779, they were all reserved for those children whose parents could afford the high fees demanded by specialized professional teachers. In the prevailing morality of the time, this situation was thought reasonable. For a child of a wealthy family, the affliction of deafness was seen as a regrettable misfortune resulting from the Will of God; but for the poor child it was due to 'the sins of the parents', to consanguineous marriages in rural areas, to 'strumous habits' and scrofula.

If they survived long, poor deaf children were seen as backward, troublesome and useless to their parents; they were regarded as 'deficient in intellect' and not 'fit objects for Charity'. Apart from the workhouse, there was no help from the authorities, for rate and tax payers asked 'why should I pay for another's child?' Up until the end of the 18th century, and beyond:

> A mixture of poor hygiene, inadequate diet, lack of medical knowledge, crude surgical practices and a complete lack of categorization combined to keep the numbers of poor [deaf] children high . . . they were left in workhouses or sent to mental hospitals. Children with all types and degrees of deafness were crowded together . . . as the medical practices to alleviate it including cauterisation, perforation of the tympanum, injection of the eustachian tube and dropping liquids into the ears, were not particularly helpful.
> M. G. McLoughlin – *A History of the Education of the Deaf* (1988).

It may be said that the history of the Royal School is the history of deaf education and welfare in this country, for its foundation coincided with the 19th-century emphasis on philanthropy, humanism and progress. It was a time when radical reformers, long goaded by the heartlessness of the ruling classes, were hoping that popular education would lead to the demolition of the social class structure. But the wealthy had become relatively isolated from the poor, and consequently less familiar with their sufferings, so when the terrible effects of poverty were brought to their notice, their response was less callous than that of their predecessors. Also it was in the interest of the wealthy, for their own security, to contribute to the effort to stabilize society, centring on the alleviation of the sufferings of the poor, the sick and the afflicted.

It was the rich, acting in concert with the religious establishment, who provided the funds for the creation of hospitals, dispensaries and schools – even, eventually, schools for the blind and deaf. The motives of these providers were not always altruistic, for sometimes their charitable zeal was, perhaps, egocentric. But in avoiding political revolution they stimulated a social evolution, the human benefits of which were profound and lasting.

Until the advent of the Asylum for Deaf and Dumb Children, the efforts to ameliorate the problems of deafness had not gone very far. Deafness was a social tragedy of an enormity no one was fully aware and about which few cared. But the foundation of the school coincided with a long period of tremendous progress in a wide field of deaf education and welfare. Throughout the following century schools for the deaf were established in great numbers and, as the Western consciousness of social justice grew, the scope of their work, formerly limited to 'deaf mutes', was broadened to include the simply deaf – and then the partially deaf. Workers for the deaf, formerly few in number, became a large, national force, and the funds available to support their efforts grew to abundance.

By the turn of the century provisions for the welfare of deaf children had been made in nearly all civilized countries, and even in parts of the undeveloped world. In anatomy, physiology and physics, most of our present knowledge relevant to deafness was acquired by the end of the 19th century, and the foundations were laid for the widespread relief afforded by electrical hearing aids. In the West, for the first time, there was a decline in the incidence of deafness and the deaf began to be accepted as part of Society, rather than as a burden on the community.

When the school opened in November 1792, living conditions were austere, discipline strict and educational methods formal and limited. The teaching staff was overworked and underpaid, and little or no training in deaf education was available. New teachers could only learn by watching their more-experienced colleagues in the classroom. Few books on teaching the deaf child were available, and each aspirant was left to find his or her own way as best they could. But such was the fame of the results obtained at the Asylum, that within thirty-five years of its foundation, ten major cities in Britain built special schools, mostly paid for by public subscription, in which to protect and educate their deaf children. The first teachers at these institutions were the vanguard of future generations of committed and dedicated teachers.

The Royal School has been at the forefront of all the advances made in deaf education over the last two hundred years, and most of the credit for this is due to its headmasters of whom there have been only eight. The first three, Joseph, Thomas and James Watson, represented three generations of the same family. All the Watsons made important contributions to the advance of deaf welfare, but it was the fourth headmaster, Richard Elliott, who, in his fifty years with the school, became one of the great names in the history of deaf education. It was he who, with other reformers in the field, fought against entrenched authority, tradition, prejudice and aloofness in high places, to secure better living and educational conditions for poor deaf children. Elliott led the school into the twentieth century and with it the theory and practice of deaf education. He introduced scientific and medical improvements at the school and revolutionized educational standards. He was a leader in the long, hard campaign for government aid for deaf education, and was instrumental in raising the professional status of teachers of the deaf by the establishment of the first specialized training college.

Today the school which was founded by private benevolence in a dingy house in London's East End, is housed in a group of fine modern buildings standing in fifteen acres of pleasant grassland overlooking Dane Valley on the outskirts of Margate and not far from the sea. It is staffed by teachers and other specialists who are qualified to meet the needs of pupils with severe hearing-impairment, and has special resources for multiply-handicapped children. Visitors to the school today will find that the majority of its students are very ordinary-looking children, enjoying games and sports like any others. If any difference is noticed, it may be that in their laughing, joking and playing they seem to be even more alive than their hearing counterparts.

In the school's archive room the whole 200 years lies in a hundred dusty books. The leather is dry and beginning to peel, but between their covers is recorded a detailed history of the school. It is intriguing to browse through these old books and try to imagine the thoughts, the schemes, the hopes – and frustrations – recorded in the fine copperplate writing. And to wonder what motivated the founders into having such concern for poor deaf children in a society where one in five infants was dying through neglect.

The first six children the school took in when it was founded all those years ago were the only deaf children in the UK receiving free education. Today there are 4,000 such and the great majority will go on to lead useful, contented lives. To them life will not be an ordeal of isolation in the midst of an unsympathetic public, but as full as for those with normal hearing.

2

Deafness in the Old World

The first thing that strikes me on hearing a Misfortune having befallen another is this; 'Well it cannot be helped – he will have the pleasure of trying the resources of his spirit.'

John Keats

The affliction of deafness must be as old as man himself. Ancient chronicles record that from the dawn of human history until well into the Christian era, there was little place in society for the physically disabled. Their presence in the group was seen as an economic calamity, and they were either destroyed or left to fend for themselves. The blind received some sympathy and charity, but for thousands of years – and, indeed, until comparatively recently – the deaf have been regarded as backward – even idiotic – and treated as scapegoats and butts for ill treatment. And why not? For all non-hearing people were afflicted by God – a fact made clear by the Almighty himself in the first known reference to the deaf: 'Who hath made man's mouth? Or maketh the deaf or the blind? Have not I, the Lord?' (Ex.iv.11). It was assumed that there was no treatment for deafness; it could be cured only by Divine intervention.

The deaf entered into human history by two paths, Hebraic laws and Greek philosophy. The first afforded them some legal protection, whilst the latter condemned a large class of intelligent human beings to the category of mere animals – a category in which they popularly remained until the 19th century. Even Hippocrates (460–377BC), the 'father of medicine', considered there was something supernatural about deafness. And observing that an inability to speak was the usual accompaniment of deafness, the Ancients did not differentiate the two conditions but labelled them all 'deaf and dumb'. This attitude was epitomized by Aristotle, (384–322BC):

> Men that are born deaf are in all cases dumb; that is to say, they can make vocal noises but they cannot speak . . . all become senseless and incapable of reason.'

He went on to imply that the deaf could not possibly be taught to speak because their tongues were tied, and to try and teach them speech would be to court ridicule. This was a lasting disservice to the deaf as for 2,000 years the Christian world was 'to live and die in Aristotle's works'.

The early Romans regarded the deaf as being incapable of helping themselves and therefore not deserving of life. The law allowed that they could be thrown into rivers or otherwise disposed of. It is said that in Rome and Sparta children born deaf were at once put to death, but as most deaf babies are well-built and vigorous and make as much noise as hearing infants, it is difficult to understand the means by which the Elders knew that an infant brought to them was in fact deaf. In later times Roman law prohibited the deaf and dumb from birth to make a will or bequest, and placed them under the care of guardians who were responsible for them to the state – though if a person lost hearing after being educated, and could either speak or write, he retained his rights.

The earliest known attempt to legislate for the protection of the deaf is in Leviticus (19:14): 'Thou shalt not curse the deaf but shall fear thy God.' The very fact that the legislators saw fit to make such a law shows that the Jews were also capable of ill-treating the deaf – but it also suggests that they were the first of all nations to condemn the practice. Among other peoples cruelty to the deaf went on for centuries, being far too commonplace to merit legislation.

But even the comparative enlightenment of Hebrew law classified the deaf and dumb with the mentally defective. They were not considered competent to act as a witness to any transaction – for in law all testimony was given orally. Even a marriage between deaf-mutes was not valid unless sanctioned by the Rabbis who conducted the service in sign language. But on the credit side a deaf-mute could not be punished if he or his ox injured someone.

Jesus was concerned with the plight of all the disabled and often remedied the situation with miraculous cures. In the emotional story of the healing of a deaf man as related in Mark, (7:37), we can see, perhaps, the beginning of the education of the deaf, for Jesus made use of various outward signs.

> And they bring unto him one that was deaf, and had an impediment in his speech; . . .
>
> And he took him aside from the multitude, and put his fingers into his ears, and he spit, and touched his tongue; . . .
>
> And straightaway his ears were opened, and the string of his tongue was loosed, and he spake plain . . .
>
> And they were astonished beyond measure, saying, 'He has done all things well; he even makes the deaf hear and the dumb speak'.

The code of laws compiled by the Roman Emperor Justinian in AD 530 recognized five classes of deaf-mutism:

1. Deaf and dumb with both infirmities congenital
2. Deaf and dumb from causes arising since birth
3. Deaf congenitally but not dumb
4. Deaf only from causes arising since birth
5. Dumb only, whether congenital or from causes arising since birth.

The legal rights of the deaf were strictly classified.

> The deaf–from birth had no legal rights or obligations. Guardians appointed by law had complete charge of their affairs. They were denied marriage.
>
> Those who became deaf after birth – if they had acquired a knowledge of writing before their affliction, – were allowed to conduct their affairs by means of writing. This included marriage contracts.

Christian charity was slow to acknowledge that deafness was a natural affliction and not a visitation from God. In the 6th century the otherwise good and humane Saint Augustine perpetuated the old notion that deafness was an affliction placed on some people by God. Furthermore, this was not to be questioned, for God's wisdom was infinite and his ways inscrutable. In summing this up, the saint erred amazingly in declaring that the deaf were incapable of religious faith since 'Faith comes by hearing'.

The history of deaf education in this country may be said to have begun with the Venerable Bede's account of how, in the 8th century, St John, Bishop of Beverley, taught a deaf youth to speak:

> When he came he asked him to put out his tongue, took hold of his chin, and made the sign of the cross on his tongue; he ordered him to draw his tongue back and to speak, saying, 'Speak the word to me, say, Yes' . . .and the youth's tongue was loosened and he said the word. The bishop then tried him with single letters, and asked him to say A, and he said A; to say B, and he said B, etc. And when he had pronounced these correctly, the bishop gave him syllables and whole words to speak. After he had pronounced all these ldistinctly, he made him speak long sentences, which he did.

The story, as recorded, implies that 'the cure' was miraculous and accomplished in a single session of instruction, but it is more likely that it took place over a lengthy period of time. Nevertheless the episode is the first recorded attempt to teach a deaf mute to speak – and therefore may be seen as the beginning of what is now know as the oral system.

Bede himself invented a system of counting on the hands; and also a 'manual speech' as he called it, whereby his numerals indicated the number of the letter in the alphabet; thus the sign for seven also indicated the letter 'g'.

Other stories of healing or teaching the deaf have survived in legendary form, but whatever the attitudes to the affliction of deafness, and whatever the early attempts at teaching, the whole future of the deaf depended on the advance of knowledge. There could be no relief for them, no treatment and no hope for a cure until the physics, the anatomy and the physiology of hearing evolved from mere guesswork to a tangible system of tested knowledge: until the legal, social, philosophical and educational outlook also underwent a fundamental change; and, most importantly, until it was realized that dumbness does not necessarily accompany deafness, and that speech is not an instinct, but an acquisition. It was not until these critical discoveries were made that there was any hope for the deaf child.

But that advance of knowledge had to wait until the advent of that era of European thought which became known as the Age of Enlightenment.

3

Concern for the Deaf

Before 1792 they had no School for the Deaf. Just deaf children in rich families received an education.

Pupil at Royal School, 1976

The so-called 'Age of Enlightenment' describes a period when European writers were using critical reason to free minds from prejudice, unexamined authority and oppression by church and state. Its basic conviction was that through reason mankind could find knowledge and happiness. Attitudes to human affliction also changed as a result of this conviction, this being due to the development of philosophical thought and progress in medical science. Thinking people began to question the belief that physical affliction was due solely to divine judgement and punishment of sin.

Generally the term 'enlightenment' is used to describe 18th century thought and life, but it embodied many elements that developed in earlier periods and which led to a period of social reform which was particularly relevant to attitudes to the welfare and education of the deaf. One of the central questions of the Age of Enlightenment was 'What makes us human?' and one of the answers to that question has always been, 'language.'

For over five hundred years many teachers and reformers devoted their lives to the problems of deafness. Among the great educational pioneers of the humanistic school of the 15th century was Rudolph Agricola (1443–85), professor of philosophy at Heidelburg. He did much to spread the new humanistic education through Germany, and was particularly concerned with the problem of deafness. In his book, *De Inventione Dialectica*, published posthumously in 1521, he said:

> I have seen an individual, deaf from the cradle, and by consequence mute, who had learned to understand all that was written by other persons, and who expressed his thoughts by writing just as if he had the power of speech.

This comment was read by Girolamo Cardan (1501–1576), an Italian physician and mathematician who made a special study of the eyes, ears, mouth and brain. To him goes the honour of putting the theory of the instruction of the deaf on a sound basis and scattering the seeds of deaf education on the field of the future. He was the first to realize that intellectually the deaf were no different from others – and he possessed the necessary courage to say so. In his book *Paralipomenon*, he wrote:

> Concerning Deaf and Dumb taught letters, Georgius Agricola refers to a man born deaf and dumb who learned to read and write, so that he could express what he wished. Thus we can accomplish that a mute can hear by reading and speak by writing. For by thinking his memory understands that *bread*, for example means a thing that is eaten. He thus rewards by reason, even as in a picture; for by this means, not only things, but actions and results are made known, and as from a picture the meaning of another picture is formed, so that by reasoning it may be understood, so also in letters.

This observation helped to break down the long-established belief that the sound of words was necessary to the understanding of ideas. Thus Cardan laid down the principle which dominated the teaching of the deaf for several generations – that of 'hearing by the eye and speaking by writing'. He was also one of the first to acknowledge the ability of the deaf to use reason and wrote, 'Since deaf mutes have an intelligent soul, nothing should hinder them from cultivating the arts and sciences and achieving the highest attainments.' But Cardan was a philosopher, not a practical teacher, and the fact that the deaf could actually think did not fully sink in for centuries; even in the latter years of the 19th century the German philosopher, Max Muller, coined his terse epigram, 'Without speech there can be no reason.'

In Italy, Cardan had struck the spark, but it was in Spain that it was fanned into flame. Within a hundred years of the publications of his work two pioneers arose whose activities exercised a profound influence on the cause of deaf education, Pedro Ponce de Leon (1520–1584) and Juan Pablo Bonet (1579–1620). Both were Spaniards and Benedictine monks. Ponce is regarded as the first teacher of the deaf. He claimed to have taught the deaf 'to speak, write, reckon, pray, serve at altar, know the Christian doctrine, and confess with a loud voice'. His method was first to teach pupils to write the names of objects and then to articulate them. A close friend of his wrote that:

> He taught deaf mutes from birth to speak; he used no other method than teaching them first to write while showing them with his finger the object which was named by the written characters; then in drilling them to repeat with the vocal organ the words which corresponded to these characters.

It is recorded that one of Ponce's pupils understood Latin and Italian, and was studying Greek at the time of his death at the age of twenty-one. Thus, Ponce's teaching system can be seen as a forerunner of what became known as the oral method. By the time he died his methods had been successfully adopted and developed by other teachers and their work brought about the beginning of the end of the old superstitions about deafness. It became impossible to doubt that speech is not instinctual, but acquired by hearing and non-hearing alike.

Pablo Bonet developed Ponce's systems into a form of what became known as the combined method, that is, a combination of signs and articulation. He taught by reducing the letters of the alphabet to their phonetic value and combined this with finger-spelling and writing. He also invented his own manual alphabet and a system of visible signs. In 1620 he published an exposition of his system in a book, *Simplifications of Sound and the Art of Teaching the Dumb to Speak*. Ponce and Bonet were followed by other pioneers who introduced further improvements in the approach to the education of the deaf.

While all this was going on, there were significant advances in the field of the anatomy of the ear. Bartolomeo Eustachi (1512–74) discovered the tubes of the ear which bear his name and described the effect of air-pressure on the ear drum. The first recorded operation on the ear took place in 1640 when a surgeon named Banzer inserted the membrane of a swine's bladder to form an artificial eardrum – but with what degree of success is not known.

The first English writer concerned with the education of the deaf was a physician, John Bulwer, (1614–1684). He was convinced that 'the language of the hand was the only speech that is natural to man . . . which, without teaching, men of all regions of the habitable world do at first sight most easily understand.' He expounded his ideas in two books, *Chirologia, or the Natural Language of the Hand* (1644), and *Philocophus, the Deafe and Dumbe Man's Friend* (1648). *Chirologia* was, as the sub-title suggests, a manual on signing which contains many handshapes still used in British Sign Language. *Philocophus* was written to prove that 'a man born deaf and dumb, may be taught to hear the sound of words with his eye, and thence to learn to speak with his tongue'.

George Dalgarno (1625–1687), an Oxford schoolmaster, was another theorist on communication for the deaf. In 1680 he published *Didascalocophus, or the Deaf and Dumb Man's Tutor* in which he introduced a manual alphabet. This was a method of placing the letters of the alphabet in various positions upon the left hand, thus:

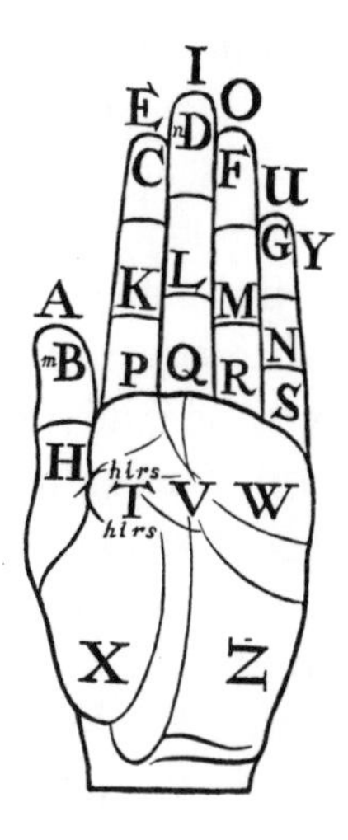

Dalgarno's Manual Alphabet

> 1. Touch the places of the vowels with a cross touch with any finger of the right hand.
> 2. Point to the consonants with the thumb of the right hand.

Dalgarno also offered teachers some wise advice which remains an important principal in deaf education today:

> When your scholar is got over this difficulty of knowing and writing his letters, then imitate the ways of the nursery. Let use and joy, variety and necessity, invite and spur him on; especially if he be young and of a careless temper. You must not be too grammatical in teaching till you find his capacity will bear it. He must not be dealt with like schoolboys, who are often punished for not learning what is above their capacity.

> It is enough for him to understand the word or sentence proposed, without parsing every word or syllable; for this is all the use of language that not only he but even people of age, that are illiterate, have.

Dalgarno's theory of teaching the deaf child was based on his own maxim: 'let use and joy, variety and necessity spur him on'.

Throughout the 17th century many more scholars and reformers became involved with the problems of deafness. In England George Sibscota published a work in 1670 called *The Deaf and Dumb Man's Discourse*, in which he contradicted Aristotle's opinions concerning the deaf. They are capable of reason, he maintained, and can gain knowledge by sight, can write, converse by signs, lip-read and speak. Also in England Dr John Wallis (1616–1703) taught writing, signing and articulation, and proclaimed it important to 'learn the pupil's language in order to teach ours', and Dr William Holder (1616–1698) maintained that it is enough for a deaf person to understand only some of the words he lip-reads, for he will be able to supply the rest from his knowledge of language.

The greatest of all teachers of the deaf during this time, and perhaps of all time, was Charles Michel Abbé de l'Epée (1712–1789) who was born of a wealthy family at Versailles. Meeting by chance with two girls who were deaf, he was appalled by the affliction and, as he later wrote:

> Believing that the two children would live and die in ignorance of their religion if I did not attempt some means of instruction, I was touched with compassion, and told the mother she might send them daily to my house, and that I would do whatever I might find possible for them.

Knowing nothing about deaf education, he started his instruction in signs contrived by himself and the children, and then went on to invent a single-handed alphabet of his own. A born teacher, he achieved remarkable success, and from that time made the teaching of poor deaf children his life's work.

In Paris in 1779, he founded the first-ever free school for deaf children and soon had sixty pupils, who he supported himself. He devoted six-sevenths of his income to his mission and suffered severe privation in the cause of his work. As his reputation spread, wealthy parents of deaf children sought him out, but these he refused. 'The rich,' he said, 'come only to my house in tolerance; it is not to them I devote myself, it is to the poor; but for these I should never have undertaken the education of the deaf and dumb.'

Charles Michel Abbé de l'Epée was the first to attach primary importance to signs, and the first to systematize them. He was also the first to compile a dictionary and grammar of signs, expanding, refining and organizing the sometimes inadequate signs developed naturally by the deaf, to make possible the expression of abstract thoughts as well as concrete ideas. For this he became known as 'the father of sign language'. Along with signs he used writing, until each pupil had some knowledge of language, and then passed on to articulation and lip-reading. He was a man whose genius was matched by humanity. His great concern was the instruction of as many deaf people as possible, for he held that religious instruction was necessary for the salvation of their souls. Because of this belief he was the first teacher of the deaf to share freely all he knew, and he welcomed all who came to him for training as teachers. He was the first to propose the education of the deaf irrespective of physical and mental condition; the first to rally public support for the deaf; and the first to found an institution for poor deaf children. Much of his success was due to his intense devotion to his pupils; he conversed with them and lived among them as one of themselves. He wrote that:

> The instruction of the deaf is not at all as difficult as one would ordinarily suppose. It is concerned only with making to enter through their eyes into their mind what would ordinarily enter ours through our ears.

The great name in German education of the deaf is Samuel Heinicke (1729–90), a professional soldier, who spent his spare time as a private tutor of writing and mathematics. In about 1754 he accepted a deaf-mute boy for instruction and although without experience of this kind of teaching, he soon taught the boy to lip-read, write the names of common objects and, in time, to speak. His success with this boy and later with others brought him publicity and more deaf pupils until, in 1778, he won the financial support of the Elector of Saxony to found a school for deaf children at Leipzig, thus establishing the first school for the deaf ever to receive government recognition and support. Pupils who could do so paid tuition fees, but poor children were admitted free.

Heinicke took note of the obvious fact that deaf children cry, laugh and shout quite normally and from this concluded that as they have normal vocal abilities, they could be taught to use them properly. In a letter to l'Epée he wrote 'In my method spoken language is the hinge upon which everything turns.' On this basis he devised a strictly oral method which later became known as the German method. Heinicke added another sense to sight and touch – that of taste. Finding the vowels the most difficult sounds to remember, he made his pupils taste substances which he considered related to vowel sounds. For A he used water; for E, wormwood; for I, vinegar; for O, sweetened water; for U, olive oil. The theory behind this practice was that 'easily discriminable tastes can represent the sounds of letters and we can put them in the mouth as a means of getting ideas into the mind.' Yet in spite of this dubious theory, there can be no doubt that Heinicke was a great teacher.

The first professional teacher of the deaf in Britain was Henry Baker (1698–1774). When he was twenty-two he became tutor to a deaf girl with such success that he went on to establish a private school in London. He taught by writing, drawing, speech and lip-reading, supplemented with a two-handed alphabet of his own invention. After the primary stages he turned to everyday events to use in his teaching. His pupils went about the streets with him, and he taught by conversing on the things they saw on their walks. This produced excellent results. Apart from that, no details of his system are available, for like so many teachers of that time he demanded a cash bond of secrecy from all who came into contact with his methods.

Baker strictly confined his efforts to the wealthy, and he would not continue with a pupil who he found difficult, and thus a threat to his reputation. In his day-book he noted:

> To teaching Miss Chichester, an almost total want of speech . . . £27 16s 6d. I found her capacity very defective and declined teaching her any more.

It is regrettable that such a good teacher did not have the charity to instruct the poorer deaf – but his establishment of a school for deaf children was the first of many which followed. One of his imitators was Thomas Braidwood (1715–1806) whose work is important in this history, for it was the seed from which the Royal School was to grow.

Braidwood lived and worked through a century when the cause of deaf education seemed to take on momentum to keep pace with the turbulence and impetus of the 18th century.

> From the beginning of the eighteenth century life became increasingly complex and bewildering, increasingly beyond the unaided visual understanding. Things began to happen for no apparent reason. By the end of the century machines were spinning and weaving, wheels were turning, and, here and there, carriages were moving of themselves. Until then all forms of motion, whether wind, water, or muscle, had been intelligible to the infant mind. But no longer was even this degree of natural understanding to be left secure to the deaf child. Teaching the deaf as an art was left behind almost as soon as it started by the increasing difficulty of the world the teacher was required to explain to the child.
>
> (*The Deaf and Their Problems*, Kenneth Hodgson, 1953)

Braidwood was born in Scotland and educated at Edinburgh University. Then after some work as assistant school teacher at Hamilton, he opened a school of mathematics in Edinburgh. In 1760 a nine year old boy named Charles Shirreff, deaf since the age of three, was placed with him to learn writing. Braidwood had no experience of deaf education, but saw this as a profitable sideline. In a few years he taught the boy to speak by means of a system which he made up as he went on. The boy Shirreff went on to become a well-known miniature painter and it was reported of him that he could speak and write good, clear English.

Encouraged by his success, Braidwood devoted all his time and energies to teaching deaf children and in time changed his school of mathematics into what he called an Academy for the Deaf. He used no existing system to teach his deaf pupils but, following his own inclination, he taught speech from the beginning – making no use of manual signs because he knew of none. He taught in what was to him the logical way, proceeding from sounds to syllables and then to words. This oral vocabulary was fixed in the pupil's mind by writing and speech-reading. It is said that he made use of a small silver rod 'about the size of a tobacco pipe', flattened at one end and having a bulb on the other. He employed this to place the tongue in the right positions. The teaching value of this rod has been questioned, it being suggested that it was merely for effect and to create an air of mystery. It is significant that Braidwood claimed that the younger the pupil, the easier it was for him to learn and articulate correctly, but it was generally agreed that one of the keys to Braidwood's success was his endless patience.

In 1770 his nephew, John Braidwood, joined him as an assistant teacher. By that time Braidwood had made his name as a teacher of deaf children and pupils were sent to him from all over Britain. Noted travellers who visited the school wrote of it in glowing terms. Dr Johnson arrived there in 1773 and described it as 'a subject of philosophical curiosity . . . which no other city has to show; a college of the deaf and dumb, who are taught to speak, to read, to write, and to practise arithmetic'. Johnson favourably compared Braidwood with other teachers of the deaf whom he had seen, and said that his pupils 'hear with the eye.' It was perhaps this comment that induced Braidwood to adopt a school motto; *Vox Oculist Subjecta* – The Voice is Subject to the Eye.

But this motto is hardly that of a committed oralist; and indeed, there is ample evidence that signs were used increasingly in Braidwood's school until, in time, speech was dropped entirely from the curriculum. Several anecdotes concerning famous Braidwood pupils confirm that, whatever the effects of his education, speech was not included. When one Lady Melville entertained Lord Seaforth, governor of Barbados and a former Braidwood pupil, she was careful to invite a friend who could 'converse with his fingers' so that the nobleman would have someone to talk to.

Braidwood appears to have had some sympathy for the needy deaf, for in an advertisement he placed in the *Scots Magazine* (signed by a fictitious 'J.H.') he suggested the setting up of a charitable fund to pay for places (in his own school) for poor deaf children:

> Edinburgh, July 15th, 1769
>
> Sir,
>
> . . . Mr Braidwood . . . claims the notice of the pub lic . . . as having discovered a method by which he is able to teach the deaf and dumb to speak, read, write and cipher etc.
>
> Mr Braidwood has at present several deaf pupils but it is to be regretted that he has been obliged to refuse above thirty deaf persons, as he can only teach a few at the same time, which of necessity renders the expense of this kind of education greater than some parents can afford.
>
> In order to render Mr Braidwood's art universally

> useful two things are necessary. The first is, that he shall communicate his skill to three or four ingenious young men, who may assist and succeed him in this business; and the second is that some kind of fund be established under the direction of proper managers, to be applied for defraying the expense of educating such, whose parents are unable to take that burden upon them.
>
> N.B. Most of those who have applied could afford part of the expense.
>
> By this means so useful an art would be preserved and no unfortunate subject be deprived of the benefit arising from it . . .
>
> If Mr Braidwood receives no public encouragement, he will be obliged to move in the same confined task as hitherto, and teach only deaf persons who can afford the expense.

In the event Braidwood received no public encouragement, for his school remained open for paying pupils only.

In 1779 there were some twelve pupils at the Academy, mostly British, but including some from America. By 1783 the number had increased to twenty, all aged between five and twenty. The Edinburgh premises were becoming overcrowded, so in that year, Braidwood moved his Academy to London where he purchased Grove House, a large residence in Mare Street, Hackney, and equipped it as a school for the deaf. In London the Academy could not fail. It had an excellect record and was recommended nationally by fashionable doctors.

In 1774, a second of Braidwood's nephews, Joseph Watson (1765–1829), had arrived at the Edinburgh Academy at the age of nine to be educated there as a hearing pupil. As he grew up he took a great interest in his uncle's system of teaching the deaf, and by the time he was nineteen he has resolved 'to embrace the instruction of the deaf and dumb as a profession'. At the Academy, Joseph progressed from pupil to teacher of deaf children. Then in 1792 when he was twenty-seven, he left his uncle to become the first teacher (and later the first headmaster) of a small asylum for deaf children in London which had just opened and which was eventually to become the Royal School for Deaf Children.

Although Thomas Braidwood had no direct hand in the establishment of the Royal School, his influence played an important part in its origin and development. His was the teaching ability that spread the growing word that the deaf were capable and worthy of education; his was the only school in Britain which offered such education; and his was the Academy that trained Joseph Watson, the Royal School's first headmaster. Of his uncle, Jospeh Watson was to write: 'His indefatigable industry would claim from me respectful notice, even if I could forget the ties of blood'.

Despite his undoubted contribution to deaf education, Braidwood has not always been well-remembered. Like other private teachers of the deaf, he did extremely well financially – which is why he kept his teaching methods a strict secret; all his teachers, including Joseph Watson, being sworn never to disclose what he taught them. This has been described as an 'unethical monopoly', but it was not unusual at the time and remained the practice until well into the 19th century. When the American teacher, Thomas Hopkins Gallaudet arrived in Britain in 1815 to learn the oral system of deaf education, he found that all teachers of deaf institutions were pledged to secrecy and was forced to continue his enquiries in France. It was the Braidwood policy of secrecy that created a family monopoly that dominated the first eighty-six years of the history of the Royal School for the Deaf.

4

The Founders: 1792–1809

We owe our thanks to the Rev. Townsend and Rev. Cox Mason for establishing this School for the Deaf in 1792.

Tony Nabarrow, pupil at the Royal School, 1972

1792 was a significant year of reform. It was the year in which Thomas Paine published the second part of his *Rights of Man* and Mary Wollstonecraft her *Vindication of the Rights of Women* – in which she demanded state-paid teachers. The revolutionary struggle in France was at its height, and it was the year in which Denmark became the first country to abolish the slave trade. Aural surgery was still in its infancy. No pathology of the ear existed and there was no accurate knowledge of the nature of deafness. There was empiricism, and quackery abounded. The only medical treatment consisted mainly of initiation of drops to the external ear.

Thomas Braidwood's Academy in Hackney was thriving. But his pupils were, without exception, still from well-to-do families. It was the mother of one of these children, a Mrs Creasy, who in 1792 approached the Rev. John Townsend, the minister of the Jamaica Row Congregation Church in Bermondsey with the suggestion that a school should be founded for the education of poor deaf children. In support of this she presented to Townsend her deaf son who had, at considerable expense, been trained to speak at Braidwood's Academy. Townsend was so 'astonished at the boy's facility and accuracy' that he at once agreed with her on the 'necessity and practicability' of founding a charitable school for the deaf children of the poor. He wasted no time and on the following morning discussed the matter with his friend the Rev. Henry Cox Mason, rector of Bermondsey. A few days later Townsend, Mason and Mrs Creasy sought out the banker and philanthropist, Henry Thornton MP (1760–1815), and put the matter to him. He at once promised his support. Thornton was a close friend of William Wilberforce, the suppressor of slavery, who later became a governor of the school.

In June, Townsend, Mason and Thornton set about raising funds. A prospectus of the project was published in *The Times* and *The Morning Chronicle* which produced a great many promises of support. Printed notices were sent to coaching inns all over the country to be displayed for the attention of travellers – for in those pre-railway days, the majority of travellers were wealthy people. Churches and chapels were canvassed so that collection sermons might be preached – and on these occasions a deaf boy was presented to recite the Lord's Prayer. All in all the reponse was far better than had been expected, with hundreds of promises of support coming in from all over the country. In August, forty-three subscribers to the project met for the first time at the Paul's Head Tavern* in Cateaton Street, Bermondsey. There it was resolved to form the London Association for the Deaf and Dumb for the purpose of establishing in Bermondsey an Asylum for the Support and Education of the Deaf and Dumb Children of the Poor. The word 'asylum' did not have the connotations it has today; rather it was wisely chosen, for its original meaning is 'shelter'; poor deaf children of the time needed protection – and their education was secondary to this aim.

The Asylum was to be managed by a Committee of 'Twenty-four Gentlemen' which was forthwith selected. Mason was

* The freehold of the Paul's Head was once owned by Dick Whittington, Lord Mayor of London 1397.

appointed as Secretary and Thornton made Treasurer. At subsequent meetings, the Committee formulated and later published, the 'Plan and Rules' of the Association. The 'Plan' is an admirably concise and succinct statement of the pitiful condition of poor deaf children and their families at the time:

> It must be allowed, that Charity cannot possibly lend her assistance to objects more worthy of notice than the DEAF and DUMB Children of the Poor. The Lame and the Blind meet the eye of observation, but these pass unnoticed, because their calamity is unknown. In many families these evils are hereditary; with some the organs of Hearing have been rendered totally defective by disease, and the loss of Speech follows of course.
>
> Surely the benevolent mind must pity those distressed parents, who have not only to struggle with the attacks of poverty, and whose pittance is scanty, though attended with the hardest industry, but who have constantly before their eyes the objects of their tenderest regard. Deaf to every useful lesson, either of industry or religion, and Dumb to relate the tale of their complicated distress.
>
> When it is considered how long the art of instructing these objects has been known, it not only excites astonishment, that no effectual attempt has been made to extend assistance to the indigent; but is a painful reflection, that many have lived in misery, and died in ignorance, who might have been materially benefitted, had there been a Charity of this kind existing.

The overall authority for the running of the school was vested in a hierarchy of President, a number of Vice-Presidents, Treasurer and a Board of Governors – the latter being the main subscribers to the cause. The first Board consisted of 850 governors presided over by the President, the Marquis of

Buckingham, and eight Vice-Presidents who included six baronets. Governorship cost one guinea (£1.05p) a year or £10 for life: each Life-Governor had the privilege of always having one poor deaf child of his own nomination at the school. Direct management was in the hands of a committee answerable to the Board. It was responsible for appointing teaching and domestic staff, and had the power to raise funds, buy land and plan building extensions.

Children were to be admitted to the school by a system of 'public election of the governors' whereby a number of 'candidates' were presented to the Committee at its half-yearly meetings, and selection made of those whose circumstances made them eligible according to the rules. A candidate's deafness had to be vouched for by two independent witnesses; no child under the age of nine would be admitted or allowed to remain after the age of fourteen. Parents 'or friends' of a child 'not in indigent circumstances' were required to pay what they could afford towards its keep. Children who were 'deficient in intellect' would not be considered and no medical treatment for deafness would be given:

> It is no part of the design of this institution to attempt to remove the defects in the organs, either of Hearing or Speech, by Medical assistance. This, it is presumed, has already been exerted without success: but it is the intention to mitigate their affliction, and, as much as possible, assist their defects.

The Committee resolved on 26 October that:

> The Friends of each child on admission into the Asylum shall provide and bring with them as follows:

FOR BOYS

Six shirts
Six stockings

Two hats
Two pairs of shoes
Two suits of clothes
Six handkerchiefs
Three night caps
Two combs
A box with lock and key

FOR GIRLS

Six shifts
Two pairs of gloves
Six pairs of stockings
Two flannel Petticoats
One cloak
One stiff Petticoat
One hat
Two white Petticoats
Two pairs of leather slippers
Four night caps
Three dark coloured frocks
Two pockets and two combs
Box with lock and key

Few if any of the parents of eligible children could have afforded such lavish wardrobes and they must have been provided by the sponsors of each successful 'candidate'.

At a subsequent meeting it was decided to approach Thomas Braidwood's nephew, Joseph Watson, to persuade him to leave his job at the Hackney school and take charge of the new institution. Watson agreed and a search was then made for premises. A 'large unfurnished house' in Grange Road, Bermondsey, was found and rented for £50 a year; the entire contents – domestic furniture and fittings – being purchased for £27.13s.0d, and a further £59.7s.5d spent on converting the house as a residential school. It was planned to start the asylum with six children, and gradually to increase the number as boarding and teaching facilities were developed and extended. The six 'indigent deaf children' were elected by the Board and the school opened in November 1792 – only some three months after the first meeting of the Association. Within that short time nation-wide support had been organized, funds raised and the school-house located and equipped; it was an astonishing feat of organization.

It was with some uncertainty that the Committee had founded the Asylum, for some feared that not enough children would be found to justify such an establishment. They were therefore agreeably surprised when, as a result of their initial fund-raising publicity, scores of applications for entry were received from parents and guardians of poor deaf children all over the country. As over the next few months accommodation and facilities were enlarged and developed, children were admitted two or three at a time until by 1793 twenty were being cared for – and there was a growing waiting list of over fifty. The number of applications continued to increase year by year until by 1820 a much enlarged school was caring for over 200 children.

The first six pupils were two girls and four boys, all described as 'stunted and from the lowest strata of society'. They were the first of the many thousands of children whose lives were to be transformed over the following two hundred years, and on the occasion of the bi-centenary of the Royal School for Deaf Children it is fitting that their names be recorded.

William Fuller, aged 11; one of five children; father a caulker.
Ian Westbrook, aged 11; one of five children.
Sarah Pounceby, aged 14, one of eleven children.
John Denford, aged 9, one of eight children; father a weaver.
John Tomkins, aged 11, one of five children; father a pedlar.
Ann Weaver, aged 10, an orphan.

Neither should the name of Mrs Creasy be forgotten. Nothing whatsoever is known of her except her surname, but there can be no doubt that she was a caring, liberally-minded woman who was inspired by her own misfortune to work for underprivileged, handicapped children like the first entrants to the London Asylum. Mrs Creasy was primarily responsible for starting off the series of events which led to the foundation of the Royal School as it is today.

It is worthy of note that the boy, Creasy, who was the founder's inspiration, grew up to become a drawing master and taught drawing to the school's private pupils sometime between the years 1829 and 1857. It is recorded that he learned to 'speak freely, fluently and intelligibly' although he 'listened' by means of the manual alphabet.

The opening of the Grange Road school marked the beginning of the 'Asylum System' of deaf education for poor children which continued for a hundred years – and the early schools were asylums in the best sense of the word. Judged by today's standards, life in them was hard, but it was incomparably better than life in the outside world where a poor deaf child would be constantly mocked, abused, kicked and cuffed – and whose destiny was usually the workhouse or the streets. As Kenneth Hodgson writes:

> It was only natural and necessary then that philanthropy should have for its main object the provision of an asylum for the weak to shelter from a cruel and competitive world. And when we remember the fate of the deaf and dumb for ages past at the hands of cruel and stupid people, the protective attitude of the new charity was horribly justified: these people knew their business and they knew their world. (Hodgson: *ibid*)

Joseph Watson's appointment as Superintendent of the Asylum

was made on a rather unusual financial basis. This was imitated by later schools for poor deaf children and perhaps did not benefit the early days of deaf education. Watson was to be paid no salary but received an allowance of £21.10s (£21.50) a year for each child 'to educate them, find them proper board and washing, also pens, paper and all books needful for their proper instruction.' He made, and was expected to make, his living from the profit that he obtained on his contracts from school supplies, and from any private pupils he might take – although he was limited by the terms of his engagement to eight of these. The private pupils were from good homes and did not, of course, mix with the charity children. They lived and were taught in Watson's private quarters at a cost to the parents of £3.00 per week per child. This was a very profitable business and one which may have had a lot to do with the fact that when he died in 1829 Watson left the then enormous fortune of £100,000.

But the high standards expected by the wealthy parents of the eight private pupils resulted in a demanding occupation which left Watson with little time for his duties at the Asylum. At first he confined himself to two or three private or 'parlour pupils', as they were called, one of whom he brought with him from Hackney. But within two years it would appear that he not only reached the stipulated limit of eight, but exceeded it. In time he developed an attitude of self-interest which undermined the benevolent intentions of the founders, and ran the Asylum as his own private school. Eventually he ceased to teach – or even care about – the poor children and demanded that the Board of Governors should supply him with an assistant.

In October 1793 the position was advertised but, with the offer of a starting salary of £30 a year plus board, there were no takers with teaching experience. Eventually in November 1794 a young untrained teacher, Robert Nichols, accepted the £30 and was employed as Watson's 'apprentice'. A second teacher was engaged in 1798 and, as the school was expanded over the years, others were taken on.

Untrained as they were, these first 'assistants' at Bermondsey were the vanguard of generations of dedicated teachers and the foundation of deaf education as it is in this country today. They were desperately underpaid and overworked for eighteen hours a day, seven days a week, for their duties comprised not only teaching but the domestic care of handicapped, often backward and troublesome children who only left the building now and again as object lessons at charity sermons given for the benefit of the Asylum. It is hard to imagine the constant depressing labour involved in feeding, clothing, washing, caring for and controlling these children with only cold water, candlelight, oil lamps and coal fires. At first the teachers worked fifty-two weeks a year, for it was not until 1796 that the children were allowed two weeks holiday at Midsummer – but even this was only available to those who had somewhere to go and the Asylum still had to remain staffed for those who stayed on. The only comfortable inhabitant of the Grange House road was Joseph Watson, who:

> . . . set the pace of headmasters at asylums. They were men of assured incomes and social position, who saw little of their charity children. But the assistants who henceforth lived with these children and taught them, year in and year out, were lion-hearted. If at times they were themselves cruel, who dare criticize them? In that unrelenting, unrelieved atmosphere of horrible habits and barbarous noises, of long toil but for slight satisfaction and reward, we may well wonder that any of them retained their sanity. They were indeed poor devils; but they deserve the gratitude of posterity for what they did. (Hodgson *op cit*)

Watson's method of running the Bermondsey Asylum established a precedent of aloof self-interest that was followed by his son, Thomas, who succeeded him, and it was not until Richard Elliott became headteacher in 1878 that the practice of taking in private pupils was abolished – an example which was eventually followed by deaf-schools all over the country.

In 1800 the Grange Road house was enlarged to accommodate more children and a small factory comprising four rooms was built nearby. Here the boys were taught tailoring and shoe-making while the girls learned stay-making. Visiting governors and the parents of pupils were encouraged to buy the school's produce at very reasonable rates.

The Receipts of Expenditure Account for that year has survived:

Dr. Cash

	£	s.	d.
Balance in the Treasurer's Hands, 25th December 188	570	13	1
Donations	816	6	5
Subscriptions	1320	17	9
Ditto towards Manufactory	42	17	8
Cash from Parents who pay a Part towards their Childrens' Maintenance	44	9	7
Charity Sermons	187	18	4
Interest	70	3	6
	£3053	6	4

Contra Cr.

	£	s.	d.
House, Rent Taxes, &c.	121	8	5
To the Master, for Board, Tuition of Children etc	1094	10	0
First Assistant's Salary and Board	100	0	0
Second ditto ditto ditto	53	18	9
Apothecary	10	10	0
Deputy Secretary	21	0	0
Collector for Poundage	66	5	2

Printing, Plans, Short ditto, Charity Sermons and Stationery	102	13	5
Incidental Expenses*	137	14	6
Tradesmen's Bills	262	0	5
Ditto for Manufactory	43	0	7
Master of Manufactory's Salary	40	0	0
Stock purchased	586	5	1
Balance in Trasurer's Hands, December 25, 1801	414	0	0
	£3053	6	4

*Which include the room for elections, messengers for delivering circular letters, &c., monthly and quarterly meetings of the auditors, coaches for children to charity sermons, sextons, pew-openers, postage of letters, and extra attendance on children when sick.

In 1802, with the school population standing at forty-three, two rooms were rented in a house in Bermondsey Square for the accommodation of sick children. It would appear that the health of the children at Grange Road was remarkably good when it is remembered that many of them were weak, sickly and 'stunted' when first admitted. The Committee had appointed a physician, a surgeon and an apothecary as consultants – although the duties of these functionaries were strictly confined to the general health of the children, for it will be remembered that the founding Committee had declined responsibility to 'attempt to remove defects of hearing or speech.' This resolution was confirmed in 1800 with the rejection of an offer by a well-known London physician specialising in the treatment of deafness to attend the Asylum:

> Resolved that this Institution is established only for the purpose of instruction. It is the opinion of the Committee that they cannot permit the pupils received by them for education to be subjected to any medical treatment whatsoever in regard to their deafness while in the Asylum.

The reason behind this seemingly harsh ruling is understandable. The Committee members were kindly and caring men, but the Asylum was not a hospital and had neither facilities or funds available for treating the aural infirmities of some forty children.

Although from late 1794 Joseph Watson took little part in the practical side of teaching the Asylum pupils, he had brought with him his own teaching methods and imposed them on his assistants as they arrived untrained at the school. Whatever else may be said about Watson, there can be no doubt that he was an accomplished and dedicated teacher. Having been trained by Thomas Braidwood, he had been pledged to secrecy, but on Braidwood's death from alcoholism in 1806 he felt free to publish his teaching methods. These were expounded in his book, *Instruction of the Deaf and Dumb: or a Theoretical and Practical View of the Means by Which They are Taught to Speak and Understand a Language.* This was the first original treatise on teaching the deaf to appear in English since Dalgarno's *Didascalocophus* of 1680. Published in 1809, Watson's book is an acknowledged masterpiece expounding as it does the genius of Thomas Braidwood and Watson's own successful years as a teacher.

In *Instruction of the Deaf and Dumb*, Watson made it clear that he had no time for the methodical signs of de l'Epée and Sicard, which he described as 'fanciful and useless.' Speech was the first necessity.

> Would it not be a more natural and rational mode of procedure for the teacher to begin by watching the objects and occasions to which the scholar applied the words of his barbarous speech; that by knowing these he might gradually substitute the words of the language to be taught; using the former only as an introduction to the latter.

Watson's system was based on the teachings of the early Spanish and English teachers and his book may be considered as the first full exposition of the British combined system, rather than the pure oralism of the German method. He used speaking, writing, reading, and drawing and natural signs as his means of instruction:

> Writing and reading occupy the first rank: the lip alphabet and artificial pronunciation are taught early in order to enlist the services of speech; the manual alphabet is used to join these two orders of signs to those of writing; the use of gestures and of pictures accompany these different materials as a means of interpretation, which serve to facilitate the explanation of the meaning of words and to help their association with the ideas. In this way each word is fixed in the memory of a quadruple chain; four ways are open to get at the knowledge of them.

Put in another way, he started with articulation, combining speech elements with signs (and to some extent, pictures) and symbols and then into words. Afterwards the pupil would learn to read and write. He was prepared to allow the children to use natural signs until the oral system had been mastered.

But it was one thing to use this system for private tuition and another to apply it to larger classes. And as Watson spent more and more of his time with his private pupils, leaving class-teaching to his assistants, standards of teaching the charity children deteriorated. Theoretically, signing was allowed only as a basis for articulation, but the classes in the school were too large for oral teaching and remained stuck with signs. By his very acceptance of this slackness, Watson opened the way for the decline of the oral system in teaching the poor children at the school and the consequent emergence of an entirely manual method. And there was another consideration. Most children arrived at the school with some knowledge of signing, and it was easier by far to train new teachers in that method than in oral. Also, Watson was able to employ deaf teachers who, knowing sign-language, required no training. Within but a few years, all instruction – and indeed communication – at the school was in signs. This situation was to survive to some degree or other until Richard Elliott became headmaster of the Asylum in 1878 and firmly established the combined system of teaching.

In 1807 Watson also published an *Illustrated Vocabulary for the Deaf.* The first book of its kind ever to appear, this massive, beautifully illustrated and produced volume remained a standard work in deaf education for over half a century. One may suspect that when Watson compiled his vocabulary he had both parlour- and pauper-pupils in mind, for he lists both earl and beggar, mansion and hovel; and it was probably for the 'moral welfare' of the poor children that he included pictures of a prisoner in chains, and, under 'H' a hangman holding a halter with a gallows in the background.

It is also recorded that Watson's articulation catechism reminded the children of the source of their affliction:

> Q. Why are you deaf and dumb and others are not?
> A. Because it pleases God.

By 1806 the Asylum was caring for some sixty children, and every six months twice that number applied to the Committee for the half-dozen or so available places. The Grange Road house had been in a state of almost continual expansion for fourteen years, but it could be developed no further. Therefore it was decided to buy a suitable site and thereon build and equip a new school for 120 children: the site was to be large enough to further expand the school as required. The cost of the new building was estimated at £10,000 and during the following year this sum was raised by public subscription. A vacant plot of land, 150 x 250 feet, was located in Kent Road (later Old Kent Road) and purchased freehold for £1,800. Although within a mile of London Bridge, the site was then among fields, with lanes leading to villages further east. When detailed plans for the new building were drawn up it was discovered that because of war-time inflation the estimated cost of £10,000 was far from adequate. The final cost of the building and furnishing the school amounted to £21,000.

On July 11th 1807 the foundation stone was laid by the nephew of George III, Prince William, Duke of Gloucester. It bore this inscription:

A SOCIETY
TO PROVIDE EDUCATION FOR THE
DEAF AND DUMB CHILDREN OF
INDIGENT PARENTS
WAS FIRST PROJECTED AND ESTABLISHED IN
LONDON, A.D. 1792, BY
THE REV. JOHN TOWNSEND
AND
THE REV. HENRY COX MASON:
AND
THE FIRST STONE
OF A NEW ASYLUM,
BUILT BY VOLUNTARY CONTRIBUTION,
WAS LAID
ON THE IITH JULY, IN THE YEAR OF OUR
LORD 1807,
AND THE 47TH YEAR OF THE REIGN OF
KING GEORGE THE THIRD
BY HIS MAJESTY'S NEPHEW,
HIS ROYAL HIGHNESS PRINCE WILLIAM,
DUKE OF GLOUCESTER.

The Kent Road Asylum was opened and occupied in 1809.

One unexpected result of the formation of the London Association for the Deaf was that it brought to light the extent of deafness in the United Kingdom. For the association's many advertisements, circular letters and publications were read by the nation's landowners and other 'gentry', many of whom knew of at least one deaf child living perhaps in an isolated cottage or remote village, and who brought its name and circumstances to the notice of the Board of Governors. So, as the renown of the Association spread, the half-yearly lists of candidates lengthened. And not only the plight of deaf children was revealed, but that of many of those 'distressed parents' referred to in the Association's original Plan who 'have not only to struggle with the attacks of poverty, and whose pittance is scanty, but who have constantly before their eyes the objects of their tenderest regard.' John Townsend himself was shocked at the state of affairs revealed by his labours:

> So melancholy were the lists of candidates at the half yearly admissions, that the public began to see the extent of a malady till then almost unknown. In some families the whole number of children were deaf and dumb, in others half were thus afflicted; cases were numerous of five out of six, and it was ascertained that in twenty families, containing one hundred and fifty-five children, there were no fewer than seventy-eight deaf and dumb.
>
> *Memoirs of the Reverend John Townsend*; (London, 1828)

Many such cases are to be found in the records of the school:

> William Cocton, mother a widow with four children, three deaf and dumb, two admitted to Asylum.
> Thomas Barnes, father a cobbler with six children, five deaf and dumb.
> John Rose, mother a widow with five children, two deaf and dumb, one blind.
> Abraham Murgatroid, father a cloth-weaver, nine children, four deaf and dumb; two admitted to Asylum.
> Jane Jones, father a labourer, with six children, three deaf and dumb; another, a boy, admitted.

When the Asylum began its work in 1792 its first six pupils were privileged to be the only pupils of their kind to receive the specialized education that their condition required. But the founding of the Grange Road School became an inspiration to the cause of deaf education all over Britain and beyond. This coincided with the great period of philanthropy and concern for the handicapped which reached its peak in the 1870s. Between 1792 and 1829, homes and schools for deaf children were built in ten major cities, all paid for by private benevolence and public subscription, for the triple purpose (and in this order) of religious instruction, material well-being, intellectual development. In 1810 the Edinburgh Institution for the Deaf opened its doors under the headmastership of John Braidwood, grandson of Thomas. Nine years later came the Glasgow Institution where pupils mastered a grasp of spoken English equal to the very best of the educated deaf. An emigré physician, Jean Gabriel Marie de Lys, became interested in a deaf girl in Birmingham and raised money to build an Institution for Deaf and Dumb Children. In 1812 it opened for fifteen children and in 1813–14 moved to Edgbaston with 175. In 1822 at Manchester a Mr Phillips, unable to find suitable accommodation for a deaf child, organized a meeting of bankers and businessmen under the chairmanship of Sir Oswald Mosley; they bought a house in Salford as an asylum for deaf children. Liverpool came next with the Liverpool School for the Deaf in 1825. A school for six deaf children was opened in Exeter in 1827 and another in Doncaster in 1829. During the same period, interest in deaf welfare developed just as suddenly all over Europe, with schools being founded in rapid succession in Vienna, Prague and Berlin. The opening of the Grange Road School had ushered in a new era of deaf education.

Asylum for the Deaf and Dumb in Kent Road in about 1800.

Rev John Townsend.

Rev Henry Cox Mason.

At a General Meeting called by Public advertizement, at the Paul's Head Tavern Cateaton Street August 30th 1792

Henry Thornton Esqr. MP in the Chair

Present

The Revd. Mr. Mason
The Revd. Mr. Townsend
The Revd. Mr. Winkworth
The Revd. Mr. Beck
The Revd. Mr. Grose
Dr. Hawes
Josiah Dornford Esqr.
George Hart Esqr.
Joseph Hardcastle Esqr.
Stephen Langston Esqr.
Ambrose Martin Esqr.
Samuel Pindar Esqr.
Mr. Willm. Lynes
Mr. James Newsome
Mr. John Creasy
Mr. James Creasy
Mr. William Parnell
Mr. Toulone
Mr. Geo. W. Meriton
Mr. Thos. Walters
Mr. Jesse Curling

Mr. William Coxson
Mr. William Gale
Mr. John Boles
Mr. Thomas Gillespy
Mr. Stephen Chesterton
Mr. George Brown
Mr. John Parnell
Mr. Thomas Hunter
Mr. James Matravers
Mr. Robert Rich
Mr. Richard Herron
Mr. Peter Bunnell
Mr. Robt. Newbald
Mr. George Smith
Mr. John Williams
Mr. George Durant
Mr. George
Mr. Henry Stokes
Mr. Thos. Dornford
Mr. Thos. Bayley
Mr. J. P. Lepard

The following resolutions were unanimously agreed to

The signatures of the founders who attended the meeting at the Paul's Head Tavern in 1792.

Joseph Watson, Headmaster
1792–1829.

James H Watson, Headmaster
1857–1878.

The School in the 19th century after expansion.

Am I a good Man? You are a good Man.—
Am I a bad Man? You are not a bad Man.
Do you love me? I love you.—
Do I love you? You love me.—
Will you be diligent in School?
I will be diligent in School.—
Will you be idle in School? I will not be idle
in School.— Is it right to play in School?
It is not right to play in School.—
Is it right to play in the play ground?
It is right to play in the play ground.—

16

Senses.

What do you see with? I see with my Eyes,— What do you hear with? I ~~do not hear~~,— What do I hear with? you hear with your Ears.— What do you taste with? I taste with my Tongue & Palate.— What do you smell with? I smell with my Nose,— What do you feel with? I feel all over my Body,— What do people hear with? People hear with their Ears,— What do you walk with? I walk with my Feet & Legs,—

Pages from a deaf child's workbook.

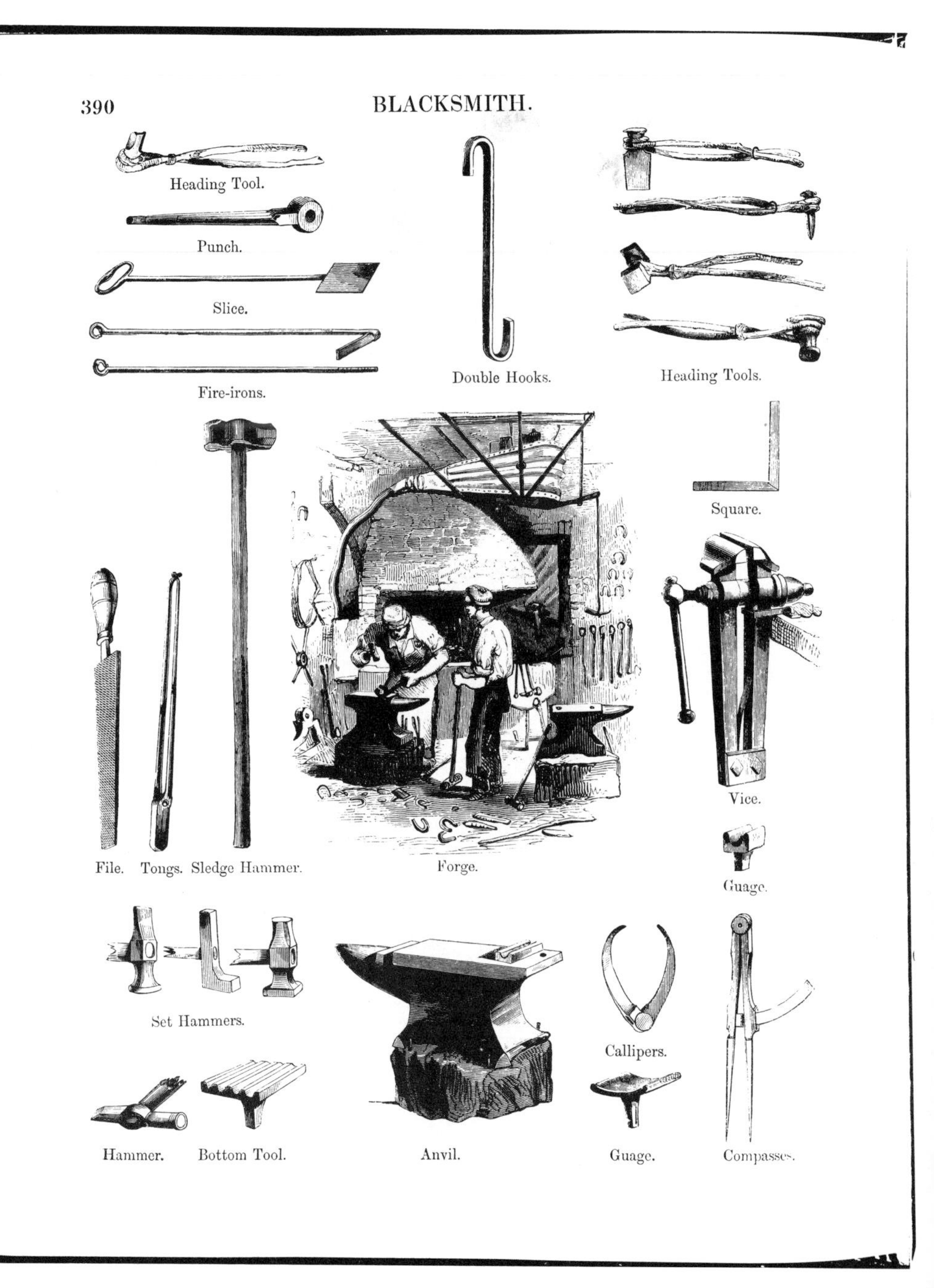

From T J Watson's *Illustrated Vocabulary for the Deaf and Dumb* in 1857.

Dr Richard Elliott, Headmaster 1878–1908.

Scottish dancers from a postcard issued in 1906.

The library in about 1900.

5

Kent Road: 1809–1857

On the face of it, people are quite afraid of human diversity and look to their social institutions to limit or eradicate it.
Harlan Lane – *When the Mind Hears,* 1984

When the new school was opened in 1809 it was seen as model of its kind, although it was primitive by today's standards. There was only one classroom which was L shaped, the larger arm, 99 × 30 feet, being occupied by the boys; and the smaller, 49 × 24 feet, by the girls. The only water available was from the well in the school grounds, and the only lighting, oil-lamps and candles. Gas became available in the district in 1833, and a benefactor of the school offered to pay for its installation; but, through fear of fire with such children, the Committee refused the offer and gas was not installed for some years.

On the opening a number of new pupils was elected from the ever lengthy waiting list to bring the total number to 182. The Kent Road building was, therefore, overcrowded from the start, for it had been designed to accommodate 120. In time it became packed with over 200 children – and remained so until the first move to Margate in 1860.

Although the Kent Road school was, as it claimed to be, an asylum for poor children, living conditions there were better in every way from those existing in many ordinary schools of the time. A Commission set up to investigate the state of schools in

Wales reported conditions in many that make strange reading today. Of one it reported:

> This school is held in a ruinous hovel of the most squalid and miserable character; the floor is of bare earth, full of deep holes; the windows are all broken . . . (in one room) was an old door, with the hasp still on it laid crosswise upon two benches to serve for a writing desk. Such of the scholars as write retire in pairs to this part of the room, and kneel on the ground while they write.

Another school was held in 'part of a dwelling house', so small that many of the children had to climb up a ladder through a hole in the ceiling to reach the classroom. This was a loft 'lighted by one small window, half of which was patched up with boards; it was altogether a wretched place.'

But at Kent Road, at least the living conditions were good, superior to the homes from which the children came – and better by far than those obtaining in the workhouses, from where some of the children had been taken, and to which many would have eventually been consigned. At the Kent Road Asylum they were well fed and clothed, and kept warm and clean.

By 1809 all the children were supplied with school uniform; that of the boys consisting of a swallow-tailed suit, waistcoat and trousers of blue serge adorned with bright brass buttons. The dress of the girls, in the words of an observer, 'could not foster any tendency to vanity either by pattern or material.' The girls made their own clothing and the linen clothes of the boys. On four days a week the childrens' day was of fourteen and a half hours, of which in summer, three hours were left free for playing. Half-holidays were allowed on Wednesdays and Saturdays. The routine was:

6.30 am	Rise, wash, dress
7.00	Prayers and schooling
8.00	Breakfast
9.00	Drill and play
10.00	School

1.30 pm	Dinner
2.30	Play
3.00	School
6.00	Supper
6.30	Play (only in summer)
8.00	Prayers
8.30	Bed

The weekly curriculum was:

	Morning	**Forenoon**	**Afternoon**
Sunday	Learn Commandments and Collect for the Day.	Church, and Religious Exercises.	Church, Bible and Prayer Book explained by signs.
Monday	Exercises in Composition; Conjugation of Verbs.	Scripture, Geography, Exercises by way of Question and Answer, Dictation by Signs.	Arithmetic, Mental Calculation.
Tuesday	Exercises in Composition; Conjugation of Verbs.	Scripture, Writing Copies, Colloquial Phrases, Drawing.	Arithmetic.
Wednesday	Exercises in Composition; Lessons on the Divisions of Time.	Scripture, Vocabulary of Nouns, Verbs, and Adjectives, Dictation by Signs.	Half-Holiday.
Thursday	Exercises in Composition; Conjugation of Verbs.	Scripture, Outlines of History and Geography, Writing Copies.	Arithmetic, Arithmetical Tables.
Friday	Exercises in Composition; Conjugation of Verbs.	Scripture, Colloquial Phrases Dictation by Signs, Drawing	Arithmetic, Mental Calculation.
Saturday	Exercises in Composition; Lessons on the Divisions of Time.	Scripture, Church Catechism, and Religious Exercises.	Half-Holiday.

Lessons were mainly learning by rote with periods of cramming to satisfy the headmaster's yearly inspection. It will be seen that no oral teaching was given. The teachers did their best, but untrained and uninspired they fought a losing battle in trying to handle classes of poorly trained, physically unfit and sometimes mentally retarded children.

Following the move to the new building the old school premises at Grange Road was retained and converted as an extension to the manufactory. Here additional trades were taught including printing, book-binding, cotton and twine spinning, mat, sack, and rope-making.

In 1811 the Duke of Gloucester visited the school and a special medal was struck to mark the occasion. He became the school's Patron, thus joining the President, The Marquis of Buckingham, and the twenty Vice-Presidents who then included two dukes, two earls, a viscount, six lords and four baronets. There were at the time 7450 governors each contributing one guinea a year. In 1811 there was a visit by Queen Charlotte herself accompanied by Princess Alice, when the Queen accepted the title of 'Protectress of the Asylum for the Deaf and Dumb'. On leaving, she presented the school with fifty guineas (£52.50) and the Princess gave twenty guineas. These visits were the first of a series made by nobility and royalty which have continued to this day.

By this time the fame of the London Asylum was spreading afar, and in 1815 the Committee received a letter from an American teacher of the deaf, Thomas Gallaudet, asking to visit the Asylum to study the teaching methods used there. The Committee agreed to meet him and in the summer of that year he arrived in London. His first move was to seek out the Reverend John Townsend and on his suggestion he attended a meeting of the trustees of the London Association for the Deaf and Dumb held at the City Tavern in July. His first-hand account of this meeting with the governors (who included William Wilberforce) throws interesting light on how deaf children were elected for admission to the school:

The trustees of the London Asylum for the Deaf and Dumb (*sic*), led by the Reverend John Townsend, have adjourned their meeting in the committee room and are mounting the sweeping staircase to the second-floor ballroom, where a meeting of subscribers to the fund for the asylum awaits them to hear their report and to vote on the admission of new applicants. Only sixteen charity cases can be taken but seventy-three applicants line the stairs. As the committee in velvet cloaks and ruffles press their advance, shabbily clad parents push their children in the way, imploring their attention. Those who can speak cry, 'Sir, sir!' Those who cannot just wave the tickets that give details of their circumstances and their claim on charity.

The doors of the ballroom open, revealing the Duke of Gloucester, patron of the asylum, flanked by the Marquis of Buckingham, president, and Mr. Wilberforce and others, vice-presidents. The president proposes the health of the patron and speaks at length on the benefits conferred on the community, where human beings are rescued from a condition too painful to contemplate. Forty pupils are then presented who exhibit specimens of their writing, arithmetic and speech, leaving no doubt that they have been raised by education from mere automata to the condition of intelligent, moral and religious beings. The president describes the particulars of sixteen (candidates) in most affecting terms and the body votes the slate for admission. Contributions amounting to seven hundred pounds are received.

T.H. Gallaudet Diaries (quoted in *When the Mind Hears,* Harlan Lane, 1984).

Two days later, Gallaudet was taken by Townsend to visit the Kent Road manufactory where he saw 'several of these unfortunates engaged in shoemaking, tailoring and printing.'

Later he visited the schoolroom where he spent some time among the pupils. From his account of the visit it seems that he communicated with the children in signs and was answered in writing. This further confirms that little or no oral training was given to the pupils.

Gallaudet was then taken to see Watson who explained to him that 'certain difficulties' stood in the way of him staying at the school. He said that he feared that Gallaudet would not devote enough time and patience to the school's teaching methods unless he spent four or five years there. This was, Watson said, the usual length of service to the school before students were initiated into his special skills and methods, and that the other teachers might take offence at seeing a stranger 'qualify' in a much shorter period of time.

All this was to lead up to the proposition that Gallaudet should spend three years at the school. His hours were to be from seven in the morning till eight in the evening with only one-half day off a week. His first employment was to teach penmanship, and his salary was to be £35 a year with board. But Gallaudet was not to be trapped. To spend three years engaged in menial work under Watson's supervision was unthinkable. He refused the offer and instead went to Paris where he studied the oral methods used at the Institut Royal des Sourds-Muets. He returned to America with the brilliant French teacher, Laurent Clerc and together they raised money to found the first free American school for the deaf, established at Hartford, Connecticut in 1817.

In 1819, the Kent Road building was enlarged at a cost of £3095 to accommodate 200 pupils; there were twelve assistant teachers, eight of whom were themselves deaf. Teachers, deaf and hearing, trained or not, were hard to come by, and even when good people were secured there were often difficulties in retaining them. On one occasion the school Committee paid £19.10s to buy out a teacher called up for the militia. Another teacher, who was deaf, was seized in the street by the Press Gang, and the Committee had to prove his deafness before he was released. But all in all, the educational standards could not have been that bad, and training in the manufactory had enabled many pupils to obtain good jobs when they left the asylum. In 1814, one pupil, John Williams, was accepted as a student by the Royal Academy.

Since its inception, the manufactory had run at a loss, having between 1811 and 1820 lost the considerable sum of over £4000 in spoiled materials alone. This was not due so much to bad training but rather to the policy that the school took many children who were not only deaf but mentally handicapped and thus hopelessly unteachable. In 1820 the manufactory closed. Another reason for the failure of the manufactory was a general recession in the British economy which resulted in a general fall in prices – and also a reduction in subscriptions and donations to the school. In 1821 the payments to Watson per pupil was reduced from £28 to £23.10s a year; two years later it was cut further to £22.10s.

John Townsend, one of the principal founders of the Asylum, died in 1826. His name has not re-entered the story since the school's foundation, but during the thirty-three intervening years he had been constant in his fundraising work. He estimated that he had travelled some 4,300 miles to raise money for the school, and, through preaching and lecturing, had collected donations amounting to £3122. Townsend was a tireless worker for poor children. In 1811 he was instrumental in establishing a school for the sons of poor clergymen, and in 1794 was concerned in founding the London Missionary Society. But his greatest and most lasting work was for the London Asylum, and he died knowing that the welfare of deaf children had progressed more in his lifetime than in all its previous history.

In 1829 Joseph Watson died after thirty-seven years as headmaster. During his latter years he wrote two more books: *A First Reading Book for the Deaf and Dumb Children* (1826): *A Selection of Verbs and Adjectives* (1826). With all his faults Watson was an accomplished teacher who, unusually for the time, published his teaching methods. The Abbé Sicard studied Watson's books and as a result corresponded with him over the years on the running of the Kent Road Asylum.

Of his private pupils, a good proportion went on to do well in the world. One, John William Love, became a barrister of the Middle Temple and later took a seat on the Asylum's Committee. Others are recorded as becoming civil servants, sculptors, painters, engravers and carvers. Some examples of their work in sculpture and painting adorned the old Margate building, and others can still be seen in St Saviour's, the Church for the Deaf in Oxford Street. Ten of the poor pupils became teachers in the Asylum and others went out to do missionary work among the adult deaf; one, Frederick Rose, became headmaster of the Melbourne Institution for the Deaf. Watson also had success in training his hearing teachers, many of whom went on to do pioneering work in both deaf and ordinary schools. In contrast, it is pleasant to record that one pauper boy became a popular circus-rider at Astley's famous Amphitheatre in London's Westminster Road.

The Committee had done well out of Watson and it was probably this that led them to appoint his son, Thomas Watson to succeed him. The former method of paying the headmaster a set sum for the board and tuition of each pupil was discontinued and Thomas Watson was given a regular salary of £600 a year with 'all found'. He also inherited his father's privilege of taking private pupils, and went one better than Joseph by employing (without extra pay) one of his assistant teachers to help him in his private work. This man had been born deaf and was educated at the school. He had good speech and was proof of the quality of the teaching at Kent Road.

The impaired health and consitutional debility of many of the Kent Road children had been a problem from the beginning. There was much sickness and even death – especially when London was struck by the then regular epidemics, such as influenza and cholera: during one such visitation four children died of cholera. It was for this reason that in 1830 the Committee paid to have a permanent reservation of four beds at the Sea Bathing Infirmary at Margate – a move that was to have far-reaching effects on the development of the school.

Since the beginning of the eighteenth century, English doctors had been claiming that sea-air and the climate of the coast was therapeutic for most diseases. In his *History of Cold Bathing* (1706) John Floyer said:

> Since we live on an island and have the sea about us, we cannot want for an excellent Cold Bath which will cure any disease.

His list of ills which sea-bathing would remedy includes leprosy, cancer – and deafness. It also includes 'children's scrofulous diseases' which were then known as the 'evil' and regarded as a chief cause of deafness in poor children.

Margate, in the Isle of Thanet, has been a watering place since about 1770. Being only seventy-four miles from London it became a popular resort when railway and pleasure steamer services began operating. One of the town's claims to fame is that of being the birthplace of the 'bathing-machine'. In 1753 a Quaker named Benjamin Beale presented to the public on Margate sands, a hut on wheels, with a door at each end, to be drawn by a horse into the sea until its floor became level with the surface. The bather stepped out of the hut into the water, swam and then returned to it. On the return journey, the bather got dressed. It is to be doubted if any of the Asylum children ever enjoyed this adventure but they must often have wondered at it.

The Margate Sea-Bathing Infirmary was opened in the same year as the Grange Road Asylum. Built by public subscription it was for the convalscence of poor people. It is described in a *Guide to Margate* published in 1816:

> To afford the indigent an opportunity of participating in the advantages of sea-bathing, a large subscription was raised for building an Infirmary, at Westbrook,

> Margate. The first stone was laid on 21st June, 1792; when the Rev. Weeden Butler offered up a solemn application that the Almighty Disposer of events might crown this institution with the most abundant success.
>
> The house was opened for the reception of patients in the summer of 1796, under the patronage of His Royal Highness the Prince of Wales.
>
> The building is formed on a neat simple plan . . . and is become an ornament to the surrounding country. The list of subscribers to this institution has been truly respectable. It is now sufficiently large to contain about ninety patients, who are boarded in the house, adults paying five shillings [25p], and children half-a-crown [12½p] per week.
>
> We most sincerely hope that in a short time the funds may be equal to the house being kept open the whole year, and not merely during the summer. We are fully persuaded that scrofula (the disease in which sea-air and sea-bathing are peculiarly, and indeed specifically useful), is never removed by the cursory visits of a few weeks.
>
> For the particular accommodation of London patients, attendance is given by several members of the medical board to examine patients at the London Workhouse, Bishopsgate Without, every Tuesday in the season at six in the evening precisely.

The four beds that the Committee reserved at the Sea Bathing Infirmary represented the school's first foothold at Margate.

The 1834 Poor Law was the first piece of legislation in Britain to contain any provision for the deaf, for in it was a clause which empowered Boards of Guardians to use local rates of money to maintain deaf and blind children in asylums. The institutions had not benefitted from the first State educational grants, which began in 1833 – in fact, the reverse was the case, for potential donors held that the public funding of education diminished the moral duty to give privately. As a result, the social conscience was lulled by cynical, or seemingly cynical, viewpoints expressed by respected figures. Darwin's 'survival of the fittest' ideas suggested to some that improving the lot of the afflicted was unnatural; Cobbett described teachers as a 'new race of idlers'; and a parson preached that deaf children should remain at home, 'as a constant reminder to their parents of their very great sin'.

The waning of public subscription was most dramatic in schools for the afflicted, and many asylums entered a long period of decline. It was to the credit of the Committees that they kept the asylums going at all through the lean years. Nonetheless, this was achieved at the cost of the dignity of both children and teachers, and of falling standards; a vicious circle was formed, for the lower the standards became, the less people were inclined to contribute to what they saw as decadent, failing institutions. Teachers in particular felt the effects of the decline for their wages remained frozen and assistant teachers remained on the brink of poverty. This situation did not foster high standards of work: the teachers' chief concern, as Mary Wollstonecraft had observed, was to impress the patrons, rather to produce good, genuine educational results.

The decline in public support for charities was acutely felt at the Kent Road Asylum. Following the 1834 Poor Law legislation, the Committee discussed the availability of local rates money – and rejected it. They preferred to maintain the old election system. They had no time for this kind of help and neither did they need it, for by then the Association owned funded property worth over £100,000 which supplemented the dwindling of income from subscriptions and donations.

There were twelve assistant teachers at Kent Road in 1840, teaching some 300 children. Ten of the teachers were deaf, and records indicate that at this time the Committee was more concerned with frugality than in the quality of teaching:

> William Hunter, deaf. Engaged at £15 guineas (£15.75p) a year. A poor teacher mainly engaged in

supervising the boys' domestic work.
John Hamilton, deaf. 12 guineas. A zealous teacher.
J.H.Wadham, deaf. £10. Chronic bad health and lacking requisite energy.
B.B.Wadham, deaf. £20.
C.F.West, deaf. £30. Efficient.
George Barton, deaf. £10. A good teacher.
Mr Diarrnead, hearing. £30.
H.Simpson, deaf. £20. Clever, well informed.
Edward Chidley, hearing. £20.
Eliza Cockerell, deaf. 10 guineas. Good.
Mary Cattermole, age 19, deaf. 8 guineas.

In 1840, some former pupils of the London Asylum 'finding that neither State nor Church had made any provision for them,' agreed to meet together every Sunday in a room in Fetter Lane for prayer and worship. This little 'church' grew, until its activities eventually came to the notice of some wealthy hearing people who came to support it. Then, led by a clergyman, Sam Smith who had been a teacher at the Doncaster Institution for the Deaf, these people collected funds for the building of St Saviour's, Oxford Street, the first church for the deaf. The church and social centre was opened in 1873 by Queen Victoria who thus conferred royal patronage on the movement. The venture resulted in the formation of the Association in Aid of the Deaf and Dumb which was the first agency in the UK to promote the spiritual welfare of the deaf. A journalist who visited the church wrote:

> Here the service is silent, and never was silence so eloquent. A congregation which gives expression to the prayers at its heart through the fingers, which sings hymns by signs, which follows a sermon not a word of which is spoken aloud, and a church without an organ and without a choir, is a novelty indeed. For two hours every Sunday morning and evening there is a service

> during which not a sound save a cough, is to be heard. A strange feeling of incompetency comes over the visitor who is blessed with ears as he kneels, but only dimly comprehends the meaning of the prayer, as he stands up to a hymn which is not vocalised, as he regards the wonderful variety of motions by which the chaplain delivers a sermon.

Queen Alexandra, herself deaf, was a frequent visitor to St Saviour's where she could enjoy the company of other deaf people and – being a fluent finger-speller – be able to follow the services. It is probable that Alexandra was taught British finger-spelling by Queen Victoria herself, for the Queen had become fluent in it in her younger days. She had also befriended a young deaf girl, Elizabeth Groves, and had met the cost of her education at the Old Kent Road School.

In 1840 plans were put in hand to enlarge the school premises yet again to accommodate an additional fifty pupils. When this had been done an advertisement was published for more assistant teachers. Throughout this period, the Committee were finding it difficult to retain hearing teachers, for the world of education was fast expanding and, after a little training, teachers could find better money and living conditions in normal schools. This may explain the tone of desperation in the advertisement:

> Male hearing teachers are immediately required which, with increased exertion on the part of those now engaged, would be of sufficient force to carry out the education of the number at present in the Asylum.

One reply was from one William Stainer, brother of the composer, John Stainer. He was engaged and his appointment was the start of a life-long labour in the cause of deaf education for poor children. From the Old Kent Road he later moved to the Manchester Institution, then reputed to be one of the best schools for the deaf in the world. In 1872, Stainer, by then in holy orders, became chaplain to the Deaf and Dumb church in Oxford Street. In 1874, an important step was taken by the London School Board. Finding that a number of deaf children were receiving no teaching it set up a number of free day-classes in London. Thereupon Stainer established in London a number of 'Stainer Homes' for poor deaf children who lived beyond the reach of these classes. It is worthy of note that even so late in the 19th century, Stainer describes some of these deaf children as destitute and 'wandering in gutters like stray dogs'.

In 1842 (the fiftieth anniversary of the founding of the school) the number of children was given as nearly 300. There were religious services and celebrations to mark the anniversary, and a public banquet was given at the Committee'a favourite haunt, the City Tavern. To mark the Golden Jubilee, the Surrey County Council re-named the rows of shops on either side of the Asylum, Gloucester Place (after the Duke) and the two side-streets overlooking the grounds, Townsend Street and Mason Street after the chief founders. The three street-names remain today as a memorial to the old school.

In 1853, the Rev. James Watson joined his father as chief assistant at Kent Road. This must have come as a sore blow to the poorly-paid hearing teachers at the school whose only hope of advancement in their profession was to win preferment – or to get a better job elsewhere. They knew that the newcomer had only to wait before securing the job of headmaster. Also at this time one teacher, James Hawkins, 'having some literary ability and writing a beautiful hand' was given the post of assistant secretary – a position which gave him considerable power, for it suited Thomas Watson to have others to run the school's day-to-day affairs. The Rev. James did not have long to wait for his advancement. In 1857 his father died after 30 years at the school and James became headmaster.

Writers of the history of deaf education have been unanimous in their criticism of Thomas Watson, but he must be given the credit he deserves for his life's work. Before succeeding his father at Bermondsey he had done pioneering work as headmaster of the Glasgow Institution for the Deaf; and throughout his years at the Old Kent Road he maintained the greatest concern for the material well-being of the poor children. It was under his authority that the first deaf child was sent to the Royal Sea Bathing Infantry at Margate to convalesce after an illness – a move which led to the permanent reservation of beds for sick or convalescing children and eventually to the establishment of the branch asylum at Margate which grew to become the Royal School for Deaf Children as it is today.

The building extensions of 1840 did not keep pace with the ever-increasing number of new admissions to Kent Road. In 1855 the total had risen to 295 with a staff of 48, yet the school's income did not rise in proportion with the increase in children and staff:

RECEIPTS

	£.	s.	d.	£.	s.	d.
To Balance in Bankers' hands, 31st Dec, 1854				690	5	8
To recd. Annual Subscriptions	1632	1	0			
To recd. Dividends on 3 per cent Consuls	2280	9	6			
To recd. Dividends on 3 per cent Reduced Annuities	1706	6	6			
To recd. Dividends on New 3 per cent Reduced Annuities	734	0	3			
To recd. Dividends on Long Annuities	39	10	3			
To recd. for Board of Children on Pay List	326	18	0			
To recd. for Ground Rent	251	3	4			
To recd. for W. Sawyer's Donation Fund	33	7	6			
To recd. for Annuity of the late C. Pieschell	102	18	4			
				7106	14	8
To recd. for Life Subscriptions	714	0	0			
To recd. for Legacies	1065	6	0			
To recd. for Donations	39	3	0			
To recd. for £1500 3 per cent Consuls sold	1325	12	6			
				3144	1	6
				£10,941	1	10

DISBURSEMENTS

	£	s.	d.	£	s.	d.
Paid for Board and Tuition of 295 Children and Board of Assistants and Household, Total 343	4589	10	10			
Paid for Salaries of Fifteen Males Assistants	991	19	0			
Paid for Ditto of Four Female Ditto	96	0	0			
Paid for Medicine and Attendance	100	0	0			
Paid for Clothing	686	16	0			
Paid for Salaries and Poundage	562	7	1			
Paid for Messenger	30	14	6			
Paid for Furniture and Fixtures	101	15	0			
Paid for Apprentice Fees	288	10	0			
Paid for Printing, including Illustrated Vocabulary, Books, and Stationery	874	16	4			
Paid for Rent and Taxes	294	0	10			
Paid for Postage	45	0	0			
Paid for Repairs and New Buildings	674	9	3			
Paid for Incidental Expenses; including the Elections; General Committee, and Auditors' Meetings &c.	192	11	0			
Paid for Advertisements	19	2	0			
Paid for Fire Insurances	77	18	6			
				9634	10	4
By Balance in Bankers' hands, Dec. 31, 1855				1306	11	6
				£10,941	1	10

But still the Committee remained adamantly independent in the matter of benefiting from public money. This attitude was maintained until 1905.

6

Richard Elliott: 1857–1862

And gladly would he learn, and gladly teach.
Chaucer

In August 1857 a new teacher started work at the London Asylum. His name was Richard Elliott. Born in 1821, he had no previous contact with deaf children, but his arrival at the Old Kent Road was to mark the start of forty-five years of dedicated service to the alleviation of the misery of deafness in poor children. It was also a turning point both in the history of the school and in deaf education generally. Deaf children and their teachers were to owe much to Elliott's pioneering work, for he came at a time when, for many reasons such as failing revenue and waning enthusiasm, the cause of deaf education nationwide had long fallen into a state of decline. Wherever he turned Elliott was to meet with prejudice, entrenched formalism and the bitter hostilities of self-interest. Yet the far-reaching reforms he brought about in conditions prevailing at the London Asylum were to have widespread effects. The task called for a person of stalwart principles, considerable energy and unflinching courage – qualities which Elliott possessed in the fullest of measures. He tells us that when he started at the Old Kent Road he knew nothing of the work:

> My knowledge of and acquaintance with the deaf and dumb, before joining the staff and teachers at the Old Kent Road 'Asylum' was absolutely *nil* . . . I do not think I had ever come into contact with one member of the class for which I was, thenceforward, to labour, nor had any of the problems and possibilities of their education ever come under my notice. To engage in teaching a class so entirely unknown, by ways and methods so diverse as they appeared to be seemed to give a feeling akin to that of emigrating to a foreign country; and it was not without a considerable amount of hesitation that I decided to enter upon the work. In all my subsequent career I never regretted my severance from ordinary education in favour of that of the deaf; and I have never met with one teacher who, having made the change as I did, desired to return to his former 'hearing' pupils.*

At first he found the work difficult and demanding, but with his extraordinary devotion to the welfare of his charges and the application of his rare abilities, he was to rise to become one of the foremost authorities on the education of the deaf in England and, in time, throughout the world. Elliott's distinguished career came about not through choice but by accident, for his first teaching posts were in ordinary village schools and later at Latymer School in Hammersmith.

Then, in 1857, he applied for a post at the Camberwell Institution and was rejected. But one of the members of the appointments committee was the Rev. James H. Watson, then chief assistant to his father at the London Asylum. James Watson later wrote to Elliott to say there was a vacancy at the Old Kent Road for which he might be suitable. Elliott went along to the school where he was interviewed by the headmaster, a Thomas Watson. He was offered, and accepted, a job as an

---

*All quotations of Richard Elliott are from his *Reminiscences of a Half Century of Education* in *The Teacher of the Deaf* magazine 1910–11.

assistant teacher at a salary of £50 a year plus board. The job prospects were poor, for it was already settled that the Rev. James Watson was to succeed his father as headmaster.

When Elliott took up his work at the Asylum he was dismayed at the conditions he found there. For the 270 pupils, there were (including himself) ten male and four female teachers. Only three had hearing (all of whom were under 25) and six of the deaf teachers were ex-pupils. The hearing men started at £50 a year rising annually to a maximum of £100. Women teachers received much less, two being engaged at 'less than £20 a year'. Even in 1873 when the number of women teachers was increased to five, the highest paid received only £35 a year. And yet it is on record that salaries at Kent Road were the highest of any deaf asylum in the country. There was also an elderly ex-pupil teacher who had been born deaf, who did nothing but help the older Watson with his private pupils. Elliott records that this man had intelligible speech.

Conditions of service at the school were severe with cramped living quarters, plain food and long hours. Elliott wrote:

> All were on duty continuously, except on two afternoons a week, and also on Sunday evenings, when half were at liberty. Any other liberty had to be specially asked for; and it was required that such absences should be entered in a special book. This also was the rule with short absences, as to post a letter and such like. Teachers were entitled to half the holidays at Midsummer and Christmas. (ie two one-week holidays a year.)
>
> The creature comforts of the teachers were not well provided for. The fare was Spartan in its simplicity, although generally of good quality. The dinner consisted of beef or mutton, with a variation of mutton and beef, and potatoes, generally bad. This arrangement continued for a long time, but after some years another vegetable occasionally and a pudding once a week were

added to the menu. No matron nor female head of the whole household existed in those days.

Teaching staff was constantly changing, for better pay and conditions were available in 'normal' schools. Apart from Elliott, who had been trained as a pupil teacher with the National Society, none of the teachers had any previous experience with children, deaf or normal. Elliott found them to be kindly people, well-disposed towards their pupils: but, he said: 'the children were kept at a distance, they must not approach too near. Teachers took care not to be seen with the children if they could help it.'

Today this may seem to be a harsh attitude, but it should be remembered that the Asylum teachers were compelled to maintain an aloof superiority for the sake of discipline, for at times they had to control single-handed some 250 deaf children, mostly from rough backgrounds and including many who were mentally disturbed. Kenneth Hodgson writes:

> And who shall blame them if when they went outside they tried not to be recognized as 'from the asylum'? Inside its wall they were victims of every petty spite and humiliation at the hands of the headmaster and his wife. They were liable to dismissal on grounds merely of personal dislike, and engaged in a most heartbreaking task for cruelly long hours. They were shut up with these children day and night. No wonder that when they were outside they tried to gather some shreds of human dignity and pretended not to be what they were. When these assistants met their charges it was not to be greeted by a polite salutation, but by a barbarous grunt and a crude gesture from a uniformed creature who was obviously a 'charity child.'
>
> (Hodgson, *op. cit.*)

In addition to the teachers there was an army pensioner, one A.

Fortune who was engaged as 'Drill-master Superintendent'. By Elliott's account, this man was a bully and a tyrant:

> His treatment of the boys was such that he was a perfect terror to them. How he contrived to escape doing serious injury to some of them was a wonder to all of us. His sign was one of the first learnt by newcomers, and the one, in their vocabulary, the most dreaded.

At £70 a year, all found, this was a plum job – especially for a sadist. It is to be wondered why the teaching staff, or some of them, did not combine to put a stop to this state of affairs, unless it was that A. Fortune enjoyed the full confidence of both Thomas and the Rev. James Watson.

Richard Elliott found no speech at the Asylum and, without books to guide him, taught himself articulation methods by preserving and encouraging the limited ability of the semi-deaf children – and particularly of those few who had acquired some speech before deafness struck them. He was soon to discover that in the face of the prejudice of the Watsons and his fellow teachers, who were set against articulation, he could make little headway in his endeavour.

Writing in 1910 he describes his first encounter with deaf children:

> After my introduction to the staff, I was conducted to my little bedroom, which overlooked a part of the playground. Here the boys were at play; and immediately under my window I saw, for the first time, deaf and dumb boys, Two of them impressed themselves on my memory. I have seen somewhere a picture, showing two boys in not very friendly relations with each other – entitled 'The Wolf and the Lamb.' One of these deaf boys would have personified the former, and the other the latter. The 'Lamb' was crouched up against the

> wall, protecting his face with his hands, while the 'wolf' was pummelling him vigorously, accompanying his punishment with gestural comments, then incomprehensible to me. He ended with three final punches, which he counted by his fingers, detailing I suppose by accompanying signs, the particular delinquency each was intended to expiate. This was my introduction to the methods and manners of my future deaf pupils.
>
> One of my first cares was to learn to communicate with the children. One of the boys, named Constable, then in the school reminded me many years afterwards. that it was he who taught me the signs.

Elliott found the school overcrowded and short of the most basic educational equipment. In the one and only classroom:

> Fixed parallel desks took up nearly the whole of the space. In these desks the classes were seated, without any provision for isolation the one from the other. There was not a single blackboard, nor other writing surface for class instruction; there was indeed, no available space whereon to place them if they had been present. It was held, I was informed, that they were unnecessary; and that, had they been there they would have given to visitors the opportunity of asking inconvenient questions.

It seems that many members of the Board of Governors required a sort of *quid pro quo* for their charity which was supplied by exhibitions 'of wonders achieved in instruction by the parading of the manifest defects of the poor children; or by marshalling them as interesting spectacles, before the eyes of the public.' But Elliott had to concede that 'under the pressure of the circumstances then prevailing' this procedure was necessary to the all-important business of raising money. At the Old Kent Road, as in the other asylums, the great work of such pioneers as l'Epée and Braidwood had become a meaningless ritual, but so arranged that the fact was carefully hidden from the Committee. In Elliott's early days the following was published in the Association's Annual Report as an alleged example of the work of a pupil after five years in the Asylum:

> What a useful and admirable thing it is to be at school. To have our minds cultivated in the great end of education; to cultivate a right disposition in youth, to inculcate a decent behaviour, and to furnish their minds with just and useful notions to keep them from growing in their native ignorance and peversion.

In her *Vindication of the Rights of Women* Mary Wollstonecraft commented on this sort of 'teaching':

> How much time is lost in teaching them to recite what they do not understand? . . . Yet how can these things be remedied when schoolmasters depend entirely on parents for subsistence? . . . Little exertion can be espected of them, more than is necessary to please ignorant people. Indeed, the necessity of giving the parents some sample of the boys' abilities is productive of more mischief than would at first be supposed . . . For it is seldom done entirely by the child . . . and thus the master countenances a falsehood . . . and the memory is overloaded with unintelligible words to make a show of.

The pedagogic mockery attacked by Wollstonecraft had long survived to Elliott's day as the basis of education of the deaf. Substitute 'patrons' for 'parents' in the above quotation, and it becomes an apt condemnation of an aspect of deaf schools through the 19th century. Separated from the educational mainstream, and maintaining 18th century ideas on patronage and the status of children, they had little interest in 'sensationalism' and the educational theories that followed. Thus for years, both the Committee and the patrons were fooled with spurious and fraudulent examples and reports. As will be seen, this was the price of nepotism.

There was no lip-reading at the school and Elliott records that all instruction was carried out entirely in signs. Articulation was, at the time, in its infancy, it was disliked and discredited by most teachers of the deaf and, although a little articulation was taught in the beginners' classes, no attempt was made to complete of extend it. Elliott's report is confirmed by that of the deaf writer, Laurent Clerc who visited the school during this period. He found Watson, 'slow and easy-going, and not very interested in the deaf.' Watson told him that 'education was impossible to conduct without signs'. Clerc interviewed some of the children and found that 'even the most advanced pupils could not lipread my speech'.

Elliott found no definite courses of instruction beyond some written memoranda which a teacher might prepare for himself – and which he kept to himself. Lessons were confined to Church catechism, writing exercises, composition, dictation by signs and 'learning by rote the conjugations of the verbs'. He recalls that in the latter subject he asked a boy who 'brought up a faultless exercise showing the conjugation of the verb 'to be' in all moods and tenses', what the meaning was of the first person, present tense of 'I am'. The boy 'immediately answered giving the sign for "jam".'

Not only were there no blackboards, but an almost total lack of teaching material and books. For the teaching of nouns, Dr Watson's illustrated vocabulary was still in use. Many of its quaint pictures were obsolete, while most by then common objects were missing. There were, for instance, no railways, steamships or policemen, but there was an old-fashioned watchman with rattle and lantern, and a clerk with quill pen. Also included were cravats, snuff-boxes and other items unlikely to be found in the homes to which poor children would return.

The school day started at 6.55 am, after which the boys had domestic duties comprising the cleaning of part of their side of the house and the charge of the dining room. The girls had a great deal to do and 'seemed to have no time at all for recreation.'

When Elliott arrived, the manufactory had long since been closed and no industrial training was given. Nevertheless the Committee took a keen interest in the future livelihood of the brighter boys and paid for them to be apprenticed to the clothing and tailoring trades or if they seemed exceptionally bright, to engraving. The girls went into service or factories when jobs could be found for them. In 1853 a full-time officer had been appointed to superintend the placing of pupils in apprenticeships, to visit them at work and to report their progress to the school. This policy was to be continued and expanded when Elliott became headmaster in 1878.

Elliott discovered that for many years no child had been outside the school buildings during term except to attend church a few yards away. Apart from this dreary and much disliked excursion, most of the children were trapped in the Asylum until maturity. It was Elliott who later arranged for the pupils to be taken out for occasional walks – although the school was no longer in its rural situation of 1809.

> The thought of these hundreds of children milling round the small playground, with hardly a sight of the outside world, and rigidly controlled by teachers who were in little better situation themselves, brings to mind Van Gogh's picture, *Le Rond des Prisonniers.* For children fortunate enough to have homes and relatives willing and able to have them home in the holidays, there was tolerable relief. But for the poor little wretches whose relatives could not or would not visit them or have them home in the holidays there was no relief at all. The Asylum was their life; they never left it, except to go to church, from the day they entered to

> the day they left for the last time. And some never left; they became teachers or odd-job men and remained within the Asylum until death.
>
> (Hodgson *op. cit.*)

Richard Elliott took up his position at the Old Kent Road during a period of stagnation in the history of deaf education. The torch of reform that in Britain had lit the way for such inspired workers as Henry Baker and Thomas Braidwood had become extinguished as school committees became ever-increasingly involved with the problems of overcrowding and fund-raising. This lack of direction was exacerbated by the still common practice of headmasters subsidising their totally inadequate salaries by taking in 'parlour-pupils'. When Elliott came to the Asylum, Thomas Watson's post as headmaster had become little more that a sinecure. He was seldom to be seen at the school, for like his father, Joseph, he was fully engaged with a 'considerable number of private pupils'.

> . . . the headmaster rarely came into the school, the assistants received no sort of training, not a word of direction, advice or encouragement was ever given to me or indeed to any of us . . . provided there was the appearance of work it seemed to be the business of no one in particular to see whether it was efficient or otherwise. There was no superintendence at all; it may have been provided, but it was certainly not exercised. It is not to be wondered at that the results were not satisfactory; nor that the reputation of the school sank to a low level, even for this time, when the education of the deaf and dumb was in a very depressed state. These facts, at last, forced themselves on the consideration of the Committee, which eventually took steps to bring about a more favourable state of things.
>
> (*Reminiscences . . .*, Elliott)

And it was Elliott himself who 'forced these facts on the consideration of the Committee' directly he was in a position to do so.

He points out that it was not only the absent-headmastership system that was responsible for the 'low level' to which the school had sunk, for he remarks on the depressed state of deaf education in general. This had come about because, being so isolated from the 'normal' world, the deaf schools had been overtaken and left far behind by the rapid developments in education that had taken place throughout the first half of the 19th century. And for the same reason boards and committees had perpetrated the old principle of patronage which carried with it a patronizing attitude to the children of the poor. For indeed, the bad conditions and inadequate teaching methods that so dismayed Elliott on his arrival at the Old Kent Road were no worse than those prevailing in most asylum schools in mid-Victorian England: prison-like, overcrowded and under-staffed establishments from which the children emerged at puberty almost as uncouth as when they went in, often with no discernible future but the workhouse.

It was shortly after Elliott's arrival that James Watson took over as headmaster on the death of his father, and thus contrived the continuance of the Watson family's sixty-five year domination of the London Asylum. James also inherited the lucrative private practice and, like his father, gave 'only a few minutes attendance and attention in school each day'.

The methods employed in the running of the school by the two Watsons were published in a pamphlet by James Hawkins, secretary to Thomas Watson and himself a life governor:

> . . . the objectional system of a pliant and subservient Committee and control by procuration were eminently notorious in the case of the first school-master of this Institution, a most practical, accomplished teacher, but whose far-seeing policy, prompted him to farm out the foundation portion of this establishment, as dis-

tinct from his own private school. His son succeeded him as master, and he drew a salary of £600 per annum, with astounding privileges, and nearly everything found for him by the committee. He was also allowed the scandalous privilege of taking an unlimited number of private pupils, with the accommodation of a teacher from the regular educational staff of the Charity, whose services were paid for out of the public funds of the Charity.

. . . The Charity is looked upon as private property and a family inheritance. How much longer shall our charitable institutions be debased to serve the ends of private purposes, because the government is apathetic?

Public Institutions, A Social Question (1872)

In 1860 Elliott was appointed Chief Assistant to James Watson – a post which was, in effect, that of acting-headmaster. He was now in a position to start laying the foundations of a programme of reform which occupied nearly all his spare time, and which was to continue throughout his life.

At this time there were 302 children at the Old Kent Road in a building which, it will be remembered, was designed to accommodate 120. Much extension had been carried out over the years, but overcrowding both in living-quarters and classrooms had reached a state where a new building was required urgently. In September that year a sub-committee was appointed to consider this problem and report:

. . . as to the expediency of providing a branch establishment of the school at some convenient place in the country with the view of extending the benefits of the institution. And, with reference to the nature of the diseases to which the pupils admitted into the school are specially subject, to consider whether such branch establishment had not better be at the sea-side.

(School Minute Book 1860)

The sub-committee duly reported on the conditions of accommodation at the Old Kent Road. It found that the building was overcrowded and 'that regarding the sanitary requirements of air and space, there is not in the present building, sufficient accommodation for the average number of pupils under instruction.' It also reported that the ventilation was 'inefficient and defective'. Looking ahead to the further increase in the number of pupils that was expected, the sub-committee remarked that when the Kent Road school opened in 1809:

> . . . there was a great deal of open space all around in which to expand the school, but the surrounding population has, since that time, very largely increased, and many houses and manufacturies have been erected in the neighbourhood, and the situation is certainly not one upon which it would now be thought desirable to establish a very large school for children, especially for children with feeble and impaired constitution, as is the condition of a large proportion of the deaf and dumb.
>
> (School Minute Book 1860)

The sub-committee had then to consider whether to open a branch in the country and run two establishments, or to close the London school and start a new school from scratch. It was eventually decided 'to take for a limited period some premises in the country sufficient for the accommodation of not less than 100 children as a branch asylum.'

When the move was eventually made it was to have important effects not only upon the school's future development, but on the progress of deaf welfare generally; for as will be seen, it gave Richard Elliott, a considerable degree of freedom which he was to devote to his life-long campaign of reform.

For some time he had been writing critical articles for the press – most restrained at first because of the danger of dismissal; later, as his situation became more secure, he made contacts with like-minded colleagues 'and imbibed the best of the pedagogical philosophy from the continent'. As time went on he became more daring, and wrote articles about the condition of deaf education in general which were quite openly critical of his own school. The path he trod was a narrow one, for in those days he could have been dismissed from his job without reason being given. But it can be presumed that his management of the school was so satisfactory to the Committee, and so convenient to James Watson, that he was allowed to continue – even if on sufferance. Maybe he was awaiting the demise of James Watson (for no more Watsons remained to carry on the dynasty) so that he would have the freedom and the power to revolutionise the running of the London Asylum. In the event, he did not have to wait that long.

7

A Move to the Sea

Now we receive a good education which helps us to get a good job and we are not made different from the hearing except that we can't hear.
John Duddington, pupil at Margate

In 1861 another sub-committee was set up to consider the possibility of establishing a branch of the school 'in the country'.

> Is it expedient, [the sub-Committee asked] to provide a branch asylum, or would it be better to dispose of the present building and site and seek some open spot near London as may be where sufficient ground might be had for the erection of buildings adapted for the proper accommodation of at least 300 children? The increased expense and inconvenience of separate establishments would therefore be avoided, and at the same time accommodation might be provided for the efficient instruction and healthful recreation of even an increased number of pupils.

It was eventually agreed as a 'tentative and temporary measure' to take premises by the seaside to establish a branch to accommodate one hundred children.

> Having regard to the scrofulous diathesis of a large

> proportion of the children, it might be thought desirable to seek such premises on the seaside. But the sub-committee is strongly of the opionion that under any circumstances it should be distinctly understood and clearly intimated that it is not intended to form any kind of asylum or hospital for diseased deaf and dumb children, but that the present system should be strictly adhered to – *viz* not to admit any candidate unless their mental facilities are such as they are capable of deriving benefit [from the school].

As the Committee and management had already seen the improvement in the health of the children sent to the Sea Bathing Infirmary, Margate seemed the obvious place in which to start looking for premises. Furthermore, although it had long been popular as a watering place, it was far from fashionable and thus cheaper than most resorts within easy reach of London. The down-markedness of the town was illustrated by a 1820s cartoon which bore the caption: 'Lord, Madam, you can never think of going to Margate'. Another advantage was that Margate had the reputation of being the healthiest resort in Thanet.

Yet in spite of this 'reputation' there was at the time a lively controversy in the medical profession as to the benefits or otherwise of the sea air to the sickly. In view of this the Committee asked the advice of a number of doctors about the benefits of Margate as a location for the proposed branch and found the general opinion to be in favour of it. It was therefore decided to find a suitable building in Margate or, failing that, in nearby Ramsgate. In September 1861 the search began.

Eventually a large old building was found in Longmill, then on the outskirts of the town. High on a hill that it shared with a windmill, it had a splendid outlook over Dane Valley. The building was described by the Committee as 'spacious and surrounded by walled gardens' but when Elliottt inspected it he described it as 'an old ramshackle place with several mysterious entrances into large caves and cellars cut in the chalk'.

The building had in fact once been the Margate workhouse, built in 1769. It was in the form of a row of small, lead-lighted cottages for the accommodation of paupers and a large hall where, it seems, the inmates had been put to weaving. The workhouse had transferred elsewhere in about 1832 and the premises converted into a 'Ladies Boarding School' known as St John's College. When that establishment failed, the building became a hostel for 'workmen and domestics connected with Messrs Price's Candle Manufactory'. With its cottages for bedrooms and the hall for a classroom, the building was ideal for the Committee's purpose.

But first, the school had to obtain authority to lease the building by applying to Parliament for an Act of incorporation to enable it to carry out its plans. This resulted in the passing of an Act in 1862 'to incorporate the members of the Institution known as The Asylum for the Education of the Deaf and Dumb Children of the Poor and for enabling them the better to carry on their Charitable Designs, eg to buy, sell, hold lands, stocks, shares etc'. St John's College was then leased at £66 per year.

In March 1862 the premises were occupied by fifty children and four teachers under the leadership of the senior assistant teacher, Alfred Large. The arrangement then was for the male teachers to go in turn to Margate, together with a proportion of the children for the period of a year. This arrangement continued until the first purpose built school in Victoria Road was occupied in 1876.

The Committee kept a close check on the running of the Margate branch and members frequently arrived unannounced to make spot checks. These included the weighing and examination of the food served to the children. One particular check resulted in the local butcher being threatened with the loss of his contract if he did not reduce the percentage of fat and suet in his meat. Other checks discovered watered milk and inferior bread.

Elliott, who had been in favour of Margate as being 'a preeminently salubrious place of residence' changed his mind after living there a few weeks:

> No doubt under certain conditions its climate is a very valuable tonic . . . but, in my opinion, the fierce winds from the east and north, during a great part of the year, with nothing in the way of shelter to mitigate their keenness do not favour either comfort or health to any but the most robust. Some people, trusting in its boast of having 'the finest air in the world' who have come to settle there have found it necessary for safety, to say nothing of their comfort, to find a less trying climate. And our own deaf children, not withstanding the elaborate care and attention paid to their sanitation and health, were equally healthy in London.

It is doubtful whether Elliott would hold the same views today.

But for children who had been herded and cooped up as Elliott has described, their stays at Margate must have seemed like one long holiday – notwithstanding the cold winds. There was more space in the dormitories and classroom, extensive grounds in which to play, and occasional conducted walks through the airy, pleasant town on the way down to the sea – which very few, if any, of the children had ever seen before. Elliott reports that the food was an improvement on that at Kent Road (by then renamed Old Kent Road) – and it appears that beer was then a regular part of the menu, for a minute book states that it was 'Resolved that the supply of beer to the children be discontinued, except when considered necessary by the medical man or matron'. Serving beer to children in boarding-schools was common in those days – usually a quarter-pint with the main meal.

An advertisement appeared in 1864 offering for sale, 'A Ladies Boarding School, St John's College, including five cottages, now occupied by the Deaf and Dumb Asylum.' The freehold price was £2766.12s.6d. The Committee purchased the building together with five acres of adjoining land for which it paid a further £755. This was to become the site of Royal School as it is today.

In 1868 educational methods both at the Old Kent Road and Margate were, as in most such institutions, little different from those in use when it opened in 1792 – except perhaps that they had become even more stereotyped and autocratic. It appears that the only oral training given there was still reserved for the parlour pupils. This was confirmed by the Committee of the Royal Association in Aid of the Deaf and Dumb, (an organization which, it will be remembered, was initially inspired by a group of former pupils from the London Asylum), which inspected the school in 1868:

> It is claimed that all the children are taught to speak artificially, and that every pupil of ordinary capacity is made to understand by observing the motions of the lips of the speaker but the Committee dare affirm that not a single one can read a sentence from the lips.

The situation was no different in any school for poor deaf children, but reformists were emerging, and among them was Richard Elliott whose writings were then becoming well-known. In his reminiscences he tells us that he began a campaign of writing articles in favour of reform in the *Educational Times*. But, he says:

> [My ideas] were not approved. My efforts to let a little light in upon the obscurity in which our work was involved did not meet with the commendations of those who, well satisfied with their own position in it, seemed to feel that they had a vested interest which might be injured by change, and resented interference by anyone outside their own circle.

In an article in the *American Annuls of the Deaf*, he wrote that despite the unsatisfactory state of affairs concerning the education of deaf children:

> We have a Parliament pledged to take action on the question of general education, and when some of our foremost men become impressed with the claims of the deaf and dumb, and willing to advocate for them, we may hope that Parliament will include a provision for the education of this neglected class of persons.

His forecast was fulfilled when the Elementary Education Act of 1870 made a start by including the deaf and dumb in the educational benefits then inaugurated. This Act gave local authorities power to establish School Boards to provide elementary education for all children. When formed, The London School Board started special day schools for deaf children. These were placed under the supervision of Rev. William Stainer, a one-timer teacher at Old Kent Road.

Following the 1870 Act, another Bill was introduced into Parliament – this proposed further provision for deaf education and financial maintenance for the poorest of the pupils. The proposals were modest but nevertheless strongly opposed on all sides as unnecessary and too expensive – and anyway, it was said, there was ample provision for the needy deaf under the Poor Law. In general the press was also opposed to any reform. Answering a published article by Elliott which supported the Bill, the *Pall Mall Gazette* observed: 'From time to time, and especially at a dull time, some attention is paid to deaf mutes, their condition, capabilities and requirements. They cause a tempest in a teapot.' The Bill was eventually defeated.

With the school now comprising two branches some seventy-four miles apart, a central London office was opened in London's Cannon Street in 1871 to accommodate the secretary and as a venue for Committee and other meetings. It remained there until 1934 when it was moved to Queen Street.

The stay at St John's College was a short one, for it was soon discovered that the building was not as suitable for its purpose as the Committee had declared. It was found to be 'unadaptable, as it was unsound, defective and quite worn out.' The historic decision was therefore made to build a new school on the site to accommodate 150 children.

But before finally adopting this plan, medical opinion was yet again taken as to the suitability of Margate as a situation for a new school. As a result, two London doctors were unanimous in ruling that Margate would be *bad* for the health of the children, whilst another said that 'sea air is not specially requisite for the generality of the diseases from which the deaf and dumb suffer'. One Margate doctor, (not surprisingly), gave the opposite opinion. When pressed, the London doctors allowed that a few selected children, 'sufficiently robust to sustain the keenness of the climate' should reside in Margate; but that a more genial place should be chosen for the new school, and suggested the Surrey Hills, within thirty miles of London. But in spite of this, the Committee resolved on Margate – with the result that one Committee member, F. Fuller, resigned because he 'could not be a party to the removal of children to a place which our medical men say is absolutely and entirely unfit for them'.

A sub-committee was formed to specify the requirements of the proposed new building which was to accommodate 160 children. This committee drew up, then modified and finalized, building specifications and set the maximum cost of the building at £10,000. Local architects were then invited to contribute designs on a competitive basis, the first prize being 100 guineas and the second, 50 guineas. A consultant architect, Mr Wyatt, was engaged to assist the Committee in judging the entries. The first prize – and the contract – went to the Margate firm of architects, Drewe & Bower. The second prize winner offered to absorb the prize money in their fees – an offer which had the effect of obliging Drewe & Bower to reduce its fee by 100 guineas.

Building tenders were then invited and averaged £20,000 – twice as much as the Committee intended to spend. In consultation with two chosen tenderers, Downs & Company of London and Bushell & Sons of Margate, a long list of economies was drawn up, and item by item, the builders agreed to the extent of which the cost might be lowered. The contract was awarded to Downs & Company at an agreed price of £14,687 but the firm withdrew at the last moment over a disagreement of the terms of the contract. The Committee went back to Bushell & Sons and agreed a price of £15,141. After more haggling, Bushells accepted the final figure of £15,000. The money was raised without assistance from public funds and work began. The foundation stone was laid by Beriah Drew, the Asylum's treasurer, in September 1874.

The work had hardly begun when the bricklayers went on strike for an increase in pay and Saturday afternoons off. The rates at the time were 5s 0d (25p) a day for bricklayers and 3s 0d (15p) a day for labourers. The strike was in support of an additional 10d (4p) and 9d (3½p) a day respectively.

The completed school was a fine example of Victorian design lavishly embellished with gargoyles and other gothic features. Within it was stark in its simplicity with high ceilings, walls lined with cold white tiles edged with brown, and utilitarian iron staircases. The schoolroom was some ninety-five feet by twenty-five feet and the dormitories, dining hall and other rooms were all spacious and airy. The dining hall had a much admired open timber roof supported by corbels carved as angels. The cathedral-like tower with its pointed spires contained living quarters for the domestic staff. The main building is remembered by a pupil of the early 1930s.

> 'It was very awesome. There was a great Brown Dark Door with 'Headmaster' on it and a teachers' room with a big spiral staircase we used to slide down. It was like a Gothic church on the outside, and inside all brown. Massive classrooms, smell of swimming pool and harsh timing of everything. PT was very strict. I did not like it, but when I left school I realized it was a good upbringing. That's why I'm proud of it.'

But with all its Victorian severity, great care was taken to provide for the health and comfort of the children. The teacher's common rooms, sitting rooms and bedrooms were so placed that the children were never without supervision. There were ample, modern sanitary facilities and hot-water central heating. The building was completed in mid-1875.

In January of that year a letter was sent to Edward, Prince of Wales asking him to 'condescend' to open the new school. The letter is a masterpiece of the obsequiousness shown to royalty at the time.

> The respectful Memorial of the Corporation of the Asylum for the Deaf & Dumb.
>
> Your Memorialists beg very respectfully to address your Royal Highness in reference to the Deaf & Dumb Asylum of which you were pleased to become Patron on the death of your father, the late lamented Prince Consort . . .
>
> . . .The Committee are in a position to announce that the new building at Margate now in the course of construction, will be completed in the Summer, and it has been resolved to beg your Royal Highness to condescend to open the same at such time in June or July next, as will best suit your Royal Highness's convenience . . .

The Prince did condescend, and the opening ceremony took place on July 19th 1875. As the date approached the town of Margate excelled itself in preparations for the royal visit. The entire route from the station to the new building was decorated with garlands and flags, and triumphal arches were erected at intervals along the route. The royal party was of unusual splendour; it consisted of the Prince and Princess of Wales, the princess's brother, Prince Waldemar of Denmark, the Archbishop of Canterbury and various other dignitaries. The procession was led by a troop of the 6th Dragoon Guards.

It had been intended to present a picked group of children to attend the opening and demonstrate their speaking abilities to the royal party but, much to Elliott's satisfaction and relief, this was not to be. His report on the planned opening ceremony indicates that some of the committee's old tricks were still being practised:

> The older children were to be paraded before Their Royal Highnesses and their accomplishments exhibited. We in the schoolroom had spent much time in coaching them; but as we knew their capability or rather their want of it, we trembled for the result. But a mild outbreak of measles prevented their presence . . . it was a respite from unpleasant consequences which might have followed failure to show results.

Thus was the school formally opened, although it was to be two months before it was occupied. This was because of long arguments between Committee members as to the particular way it should be used – and how it should be run.

Evidentially the Committee was beginning to have some doubts about the overall management of the two schools. Eventually they agreed that the new school's teaching curriculum was to be divided into three departments; Junior, Intermediate and Senior – the last being for pupils over the age of thirteen. A special class was provided for semi-deaf pupils, and another for those considered backward. But the most important and far-reaching decision was that the Margate establishment was not to be managed by James Watson, but would have its own headmaster. This resolution implied strong criticism of Watson's methods and attitudes and was to develop into another major turning point in the history of the school.

Advertisements for applications to fill the post of headmaster were placed in all the principal UK papers – although it is more probable that some enlightened members of the Committee already had Richard Elliott in mind for the job. There were a great many applications and Elliott's name was among them; it was also included in the short list of five which was selected. Each of these candidates was required to write a 'scheme of instruction and management' for the new institution. Elliott's 'scheme' embodied all the principals he had been fighting for since he joined the school in 1857, and all of which he lived to see fulfilled. The changes he proposed in the running of the school were, in his own words, 'for the sake of the better graduating of the instruction, for inducing emulation, and for other reasons.' They included:

> the teaching of the boys and girls in the same classes; the making provision for the isolation of the respective classes [ie oral and signing]; the providing of some [more] class-rooms; the arrangement of a definite system in teaching all the subjects; the teaching of drawing as in the elementary schools; the discouragement of signing as a means of ordinary intercourse; the giving of prizes as an acknowledgement of an encouragement for progress; the institution of a pupil-teacher system for training teachers; periodical examinations from both within and without the school.
>
> (*Reminiscences*...,Elliott)

By 'oral' Elliott meant the 'combined systems' of training – ie, the combination of signing, lipreading and articulation – which he had championed for years but with little success.

The Committee complimented Elliott on his 'scheme' and asked him if he were 'competent to carry it out'. He replied that he was, and, in February, learned that he had the job. The new school was to be occupied in 1876 with ninety boys and sixty girls.

Elliott's scheme referred to the need for a 'definite system of instruction in all subjects'. In his *Reminiscences,* he enlarges upon this:

> There are so many points needing attention in a subject, and so many divergent views as to the best way

> of dealing with them, that if there is not a standard course adopted to work by, some essential features will be overlooked. I know a great deal is said in favour of hap-hazard teaching, and of such indirect measures as are so well adapted for the 'hearing', and much is made of the greater diffusion in the practice of oral speech and of finger-spelling than formally existed; and of the advantages which the swarms of attractively illustrated lesson and other books will give; but with all these I hold that there is still the same need for direct elementary instruction in language as formally existed. How many bright children have come to us, already partly instructed, who with a superficial jabber in short disjointed sentences on a few stock subjects, had absolutely no ability to express the simplest matter in an intelligible form!

The appointment as head of Margate gave Elliott a considerable degree of freedom from Watson and therefore the opportunity to begin his long-planned, long-term reforms.

> For this burden he had both the ability, the energy, and the courage. He had, moreover, the savage grace of humour and tact, which enabled him to mature his plans and take the first critical steps without losing either his equanimity or his job.
>
> (Hodgson *op. cit.*)

Elliott himself remarks on the tolerance his efforts were now receiving from the Committee:

> Among my recommendations was one suggesting that the Master appointed should make visits of inspection to some of the principal Provincial schools, and report to the Committee upon them, in order to see if any of their methods and proceedings might be advantageously

> adopted. To have proposed such a thing a few years before would have been considered to be an extreme and bold suggestion. The traditional view with which the Old Kent Road Asylum had for long been credited was exclusive self-sufficiency; and it was the general opinion that it claimed almost a monopoly of the work of benefiting the deaf. But this was far from being the case; progress and improvement were now the order of the day; my suggestion was received with favour and my wish freely granted.

With time to spare before the occupation of the new building, Elliott went off on a tour of schools for the deaf in Liverpool, Manchester, Newcastle, Doncaster and Birmingham to study the progress of the oral method which was then attracting increasing attention in the field of deaf education. Elliott, long a critic of the conservative attitude to this system, was surprised to find that articulation was hardly taught at all, except at the Doncaster Institute for the Deaf and Dumb. Here the headmaster, James Howard, had strongly opposed the oral system until being converted by Abba Balestra who had recently visited his school. Balestra (1834–86), was a distinguished Italian teacher and an energetic champion of the oral system. Having changed the views of many teachers in Italy, he went to several other countries to advocate and demonstrate the method. One of his visits was to the Old Kent Road in 1876 where he enthused about the oral system – only to be shown the door by James Watson who had no wish for any changes. The meeting between Richard Elliott and James Howard was to have important consequences in deaf education.

At none of the schools did Elliott find any system of examinations, other than the usual public exhibitions given to satisfy patrons or to raise funds. He found that the living conditions of assistant teachers made no provision for 'comfort or convenience.' Yet he was surprised to find that:

> . . . arrangements for walks and relaxation were satis-

> factory; with much more liberty than was allowed in London, and much more than I could, for a long time, get at Margate, where the view was that no child should be allowed out of the Institution except in the company of an official.

Elliott also found that the old workhouse atmosphere of deaf institutions was fast improving, most of the schools being 'attractive in appearance'.

Elliott found he had a staunch ally for his ideas in James Howard. Together the two men planned and organized support for a Conference of Principals of Deaf Institutions to be held in 1877 at the premises of the Social Sciences Association, of which Elliott was secretary. There had been two such conferences earlier – in 1851 and 1852, but they had simply condemned articulation – this being the very opposite of what Elliott was now advocating. Elliott invited James Watson to attend the proposed conference but Watson did not bother to reply. He was in fact behind the resolution passed by the Committee of the Old Kent Road that Elliott's participation in the conference was 'very distasteful.' This was meant to dissuade Elliott from having anything to do with the meeting, but needless to say he went. Some eighty people attended, mainly principals of schools, but including many influential advocates of the oral method. A number of subjects were discussed, such as the advantages of small classes, the state of deaf education and the question of state aid for institutions – the latter being dealt with in a paper by Elliott. But the main topic was oral teaching, and for this there was strong support. Participants in the meeting were persuaded to visit a notable private school for the deaf at Notting Hill to see what skilled oral teaching could do. Here they were so impressed that they resolved that teaching methods in all the institutions were due for reform. They were also unanimous that state aid for deaf education was long overdue.

There can be no doubt that in organizing this conference,

Elliott and Howard sparked off a process which resulted in the emergence of a new order and the decline of the old. But to all this, and other progress, a hard core of teachers at the established asylums remained obstinately unmoved.

In 1876, the new Margate building was occupied by the ninety boys and sixty girls. The teaching staff included three boys and three girls who had been recruited as pupil-teachers; one boy and one girl were deaf. It is a credit to the school that one of the boy pupil-teachers became famous in his time for his Mission work for the deaf, and another well-known as a teacher in a leading American school for the deaf.

The reforming resolutions of the Conference of 1877 had seemed like heresy to old James Watson in his citadel at the Old Kent Road, and rather than be responsible for leading his school into the new era – which even he could see was inevitable – he resigned in the following year after twenty-six years with the Asylum – twenty-one of them as headmaster. He was the first of his family to do so, for the others had died in harness. James Watson's departure was the end of the eighty-six year reign of the Watson family. Richard Elliott was then appointed head of both the London and the Margate schools and the Committee, in the absence of Watson, withdrew its condemnation of the previous year. Elliott was given no increase in his salary but received what he described as 'a gratuity voted to me from time to time.' Neither did the Committee provide him with living accommodation – probably because it did not want a continuation of the Watson practice of taking in private pupils.

At last Elliott had a free hand to continue to implement his ideas. Under Watson's direction the school used no connected graduated system of teaching and in London no systematic speech-training existed. Elliott's first moves were tentative and to a large degree experimental; he had no model to follow, for no other schools were working in a similar direction:

> There was a good deal of inertia to overcome before any reasonable rate of progress could be secured. So,

measures might be proposed, and improvements suggested, only to be passed by unheeded, or practically condemned, by faint praise. Possibilities were not recognized, and there was no appreciation of proposed remedies.

(*Reminiscences*. . ., Elliott)

His first move was to reorganize the school as a whole into two departments, London and Margate, so as to have uniformity in teaching methods. He then systemized and graduated the methods of instruction. As the majority of the staff consisted of young, inexperienced teachers, Elliott himself composed manuals on the teaching of the combined system. One was on the use of signing and spelling; one on articulation, and another on the teaching of scripture. Not having the money to get them printed he bought a small hand press and produced them himself.

Another reform was to unite the boys and girls classes – although out of the classroom the children were, in Elliott's words, 'strictly supervised so as not to converse together'. This was to prevent them from 'forming attachments' which might have led to marriage – and the possibility of deaf offspring. But even in the classroom, this mingling of boys and girls was a situation that Watson would never have allowed. Elliott also introduced a system whereby his trainee teachers at Margate were bound to complete a three year course. These reforms were minor and tentative, but they were the beginning of greater changes to come.

Elliott also eased the strict discipline that had become a tradition in institutions and did much to improve teacher/pupil relationships. In his *Reminiscences* he wrote:

Our school was bright and new, as was all the furniture. The school-room itself was long and narrow . . . and the outlook was pleasant. We felt a pride in our pleasant surroundings. Our children became more and more objects of interest to all of us; the old

> stand-offishness of which I had seen so much formerly, seemed to disappear, and attachment – even affection – between teacher and pupil grew up and became the ruling principle. This is not a thing now to be noted as exceptional, but it is to be found everywhere; and it is one of the developments of our work which I look upon with the greatest of pleasure. To see how close is now the tie between deaf pupil and teacher, and to recognize the intensity of the desire on the part of the latter to benefit his charge, cannot but be gratifying to us all.

The results of the new methods were described in an article which appeared in *The Daily Telegraph* in 1879 – probably the earliest article to appear in a national newspaper which described the actual teaching of the deaf. The reporter was so impressed with what he saw that he headed his article 'A Modern Miracle' and said:

> Without infinite patience, and a success which is like a triumph of humanity, they literally make the dumb to speak . . . [in the playground] the prettiest sight of all was that of the girls flocking round their master with boldness and affection...following him to the door in a very whirl of hands and fingers. The work done at Margate is all that can be desired.

Within four years of taking over at Margate, Elliott had succeeded in putting many of his reforms into practice, and the Committee was able to report that 'an effort is made to give *every child* the benefit of learning to articulate and read from the lips'.

In an examination of all the children at both schools at about this time, an inspector found that many of the children at Margate could lipread and speak intelligibly, and had attained a standard of education comparable with hearing children of the same age.

> Articulation: the results in a few cases are remarkable. One boy only five months at the school can say 'a piece of cake' in a perfectly intelligible manner, and almost any other simple word; while another can repeat intelligibly the whole of the Lord's Prayer.
>
> Writing: Remarkably good and neat throughout.
>
> Arithmetic: Very good throughout the school. The class, two years in the school, work up to compound addition and passed sixteen out of seventeen.

In 1879 the decision was taken to further enlarge the Margate school with an additional building. This was a result of the noticeable improvement in the physical health of many of those children who were weak and ailing, on their arrival at Margate. In May 1880, all the Margate children, ailing or otherwise were moved back and packed into the old London school whilst the extensions and improvements were carried out. In July of that year the foundation stone of the additional building was laid by Sir Francis Truscott, the Lord Mayor of London and the enlarged school reoccupied in March 1881.

During the two-year period of the building operations there were some far-reaching developments in deaf education. In 1878 there had occurred in Paris the first International Conference of Teachers of the Deaf. Elliott, who was there, says that 'the conference was international in name only and that little of immediate value was achieved.' But one achievement was an agreement to hold another conference two years later. When it occurred, this event was indeed international and was an important milestone in the development of deaf education throughout the world. This was the International Congress on the Education of the Deaf which took place in Milan in 1880. It resulted in some drastic changes in many aspects of deaf education that were long overdue. But its main concern was a subject that had been of growing interest among teachers of the deaf for many years.

Royal School for Deaf and Dumb Children
Margate

Certificate
of
General Usefulness

This is to Certify that

has obtained at least 75 per cent. of Marks in each of the following requirements:

Sole and heel boots.
Take measurements.
Repair trousers bottoms.
Repair coat cuffs.
Patch coat lining.
Darn socks.
Plane up a piece of wood true.
Grind and sharpen a knife.
Put in a pane of glass.
Fix a hinge and a lock.
Make an Oxford picture frame.
Repair a sash-line.
Dig a plot of ground.
Go errands.
Give and receive correct change.
Swim a distance.

Signed
Headmaster

Royal School for Deaf and Dumb Children
Margate

Certificate
of
General Usefulness

This is to Certify that

has obtained at least 75 per cent. of Marks in each of the following requirements:

Cut out and make under-garment.
Patch a garment.
Use the sewing machine.
Take measurements.
Knit a garment.
Darn a sock.
Wash and iron an under-garment and an apron.
Clean the kitchen range and flues.
Lay a fire.
Cook a joint, potatoes, vegetables.
Make soup, three kinds of pudding.
Cook eggs in three different ways.
Set a table for dinner and tea.
Make a bed and turn out bedroom.
Bath and dress an infant.
Bandage a finger.
Go errands.
Give and receive correct change.
Swim a distance.

Signed
Headmaster

Certificates of General Usefulness – for Boys (top) and Girls (bottom).

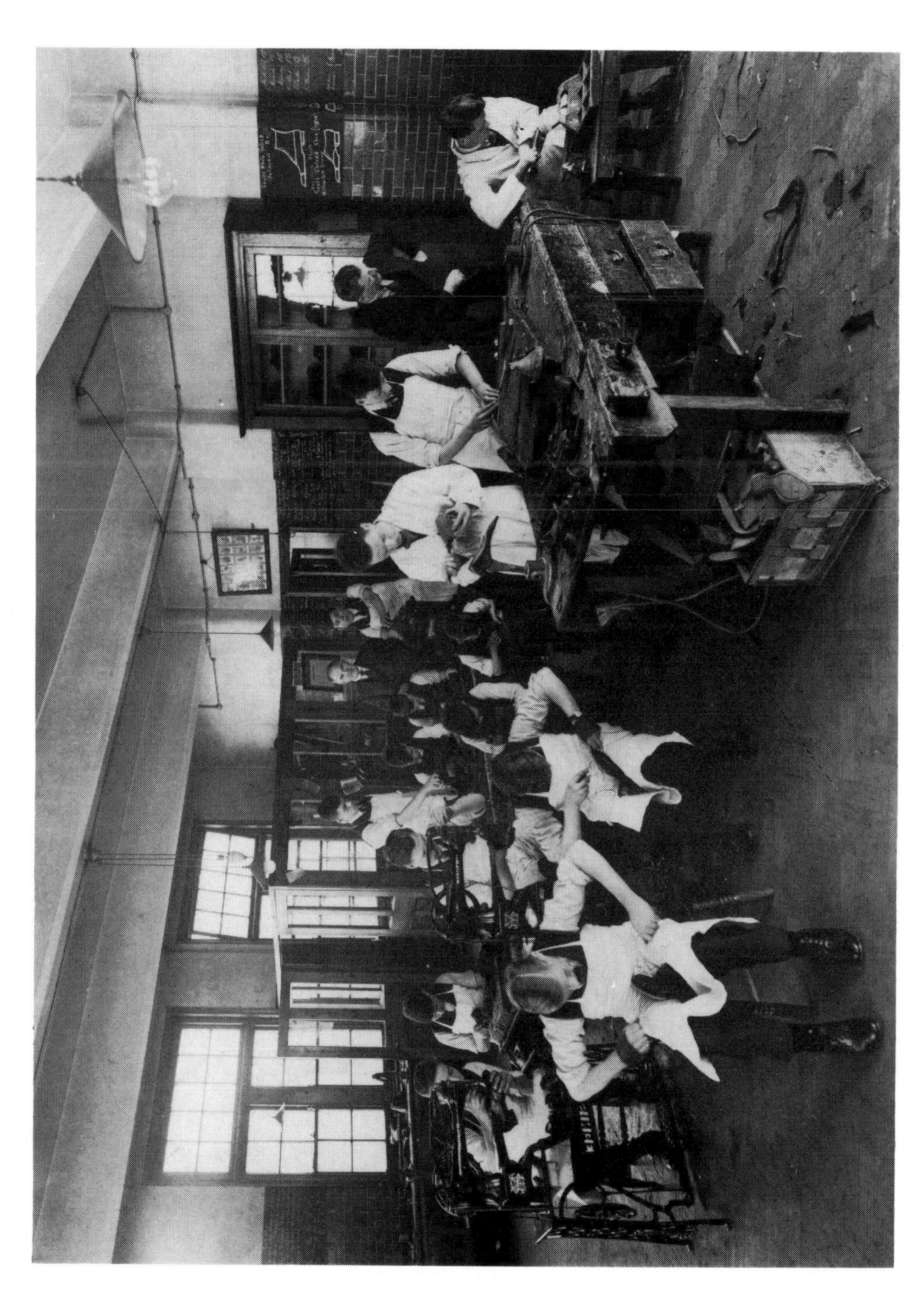

Boot repairs (about 1912).

The laundry (about 1912).

A dormitory (about 1912).

The dining hall (about 1912).

The School Dietary.

BREAKFAST.

Varied daily with bread and dripping or butter, and with coffee or cocoa or milk.

DINNER.

Selected daily from :—

1. Hot roast or boiled meat with potatoes, greens and bread, baked rice pudding.

2. Boiled bacon with beans, potatoes and bread, milk pudding.

3. Cold meat with salad in season, potatoes (except on Sundays) and bread, plain pudding and stewed fruit.

4. Meat and potato pie with bread, milk pudding.

5. Meat pie with crust, potatoes and greens, milk pudding.

6. Irish stew with potatoes and bread, suet pudding with jam or sugar.

7. Meat pudding with greens, potatoes and bread, milk pudding.

8. Shepherd's pie, with turnips and bread, steamed rice with jam, treacle or sugar.

9. Fish and potatoes with bread, baked bread pudding.

10. Soup (pea, lentil, potato), or Scotch broth with bread, raisin or currant pudding.

TEA.

Varied daily with bread and butter or jam, and with tea or cocoa.

SUPPER.

Biscuits.

NOTE.—A lunch is also provided for delicate pupils at 10.30 a.m.

A page from the Royal School Magazine in 1915 showing the school menu.

Dressmaking instruction in Goring-on-Thames during the evacuation in the Second World War.

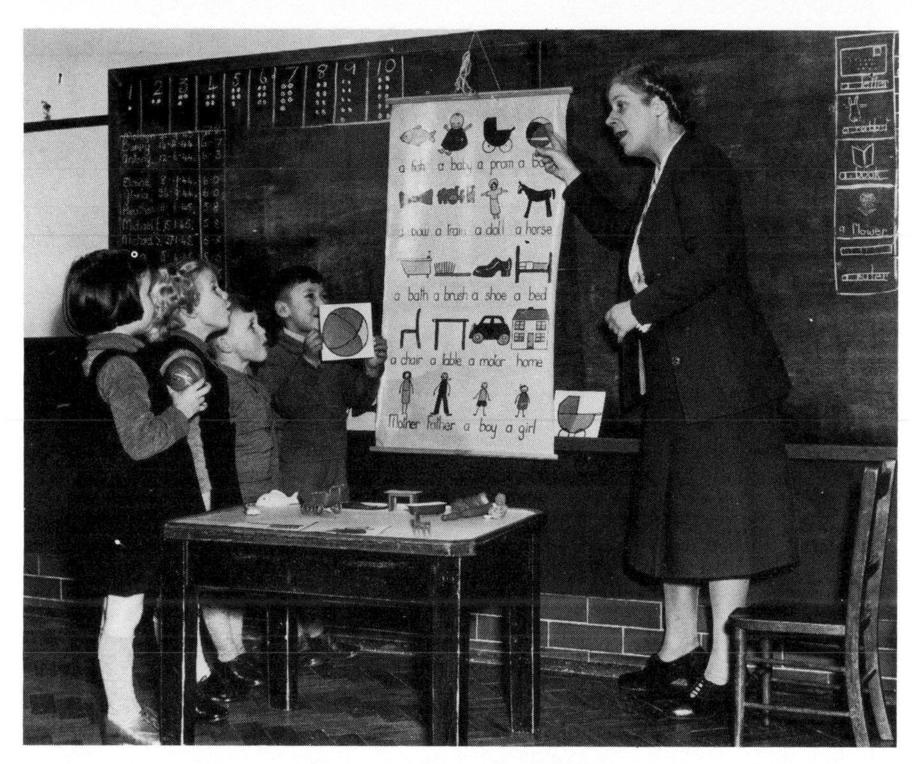

Language lesson in the 50s.

Children shown using post-war army surplus headsets.

8

The Great Controversy

It is quite natural. Some hear more pleasantly with the eyes than with the ears. I do.
Gertrude Stein

Ever since Heinicke introduced his system of oral training in the middle of the 18th century, there had been a lively controversy between exponents of the two different methods of teaching the deaf – the 'pure oral' method and the signing and finger-spelling method. It is a controversy that, to some extent, continues today.

In the widest sense of the word, language is the means of communication between living beings, for there is no doubt that many animals have the means of communicating thoughts and feelings. But in its developed form it is an exclusively human characteristic and the chief distinctive mark of humanity. It is one of the most potent forces in social life; it welds communities together and makes them more than just a number of isolated individuals. Not even the most primitive tribe lacks language and every language must have behind it a history of many thousands of years. But language is by no means limited to sounds.

Speech as a mode of human intercourse is normally used between persons who are in visible contact. Therefore the gestures, facial expressions, bodily movements of the two parties are integral, if not essential, elements in the intercourse. Thus 'when the postural tensions and the spoken word contradict each other it is plain which should be given credence.'* It follows, therefore, that when two parties are in visible contact there is always an element of natural gesture in their speech. Leonardo da Vinci noted the importance of bodily gesture in conversation:

> . . . a deaf mute, who sees two people talking, although himself deprived of the power of hearing, is none the less able to divine from the movements and gestures of the speakers the subject of their discussion.

The traveller J.H. Hutton describes a deaf person who in signs made 'a long detailed complaint of an assault in which nothing was missing except proper names and even these were eventually identified by means of the man's description of his assailant's dress and personal appearance.'

Spoken language is not always fully adopted by society. Some American Indian tribes developed a gesture language of their own which they used – and still use – in preference to the spoken word. In the 15th century it was found that between them the North American Indian tribes spoke some 500 different languages, and to overcome the absence of a common tongue they had contrived 'Hand Talk' which was readily understood between them all. In 1880 one group of Indians were taken to a school for American deaf children in Washington. Both the Indians and the children used their own sign language and were easily able to communicate with one another. In the Middle Ages many Guilds used signs in their rituals and as a means of identification, and such signs are still used by groups such as the Freemasons. There are religious communities existing today whose order forbids them to speak or write, and who have used sign language for centuries. Trappist monks, for example, who are forbidden even to write, have developed a complex system of

*W.A.White, *Foundations of Psychiatry* 1921.

signs to communicate with each other.

With their lack of inhibition, young children express themselves with their whole bodies by jumping for joy and stamping in anger. Deaf children do the same, and if they are thrown together in each other's company they will invariably, and without formal training, develop their own system of signs. This comes naturally, for the use of signs makes conversation more rapid, and is not so tiring to the eyes as constant finger-spelling.

It is to the great teacher of the deaf de l'Epée that belongs the credit of developing the crude gestures of the untrained deaf into a beautiful language almost as conventional as other languages. His method was further developed and improved by his successors in France so that in time signing became known as the French system. Over the years it made such progress that deaf people taught by the method could carry on intelligent conversation together almost as easily as the spoken.

Signs fall into four main categories:

1. Of emotions, facial expressions etc.
2. Dramatic, as used in oratory and to emphasize meanings of words.
3. Imitative; ie. natural pantomime.
4. Symbolic, or conventional signs; these are generally imitative but symbolic of something else.

The grand principle which lies at the bottom of gestures and signs is resemblance. With a few exceptions, words are entirely arbitrary in their meaning, and bear no likeness to the objects or ideas they represent – but signs are nothing without a resemblance, more or less apparent, to the thing signified. The untrained deaf child instinctively seeks, and invariably finds, some likeness which by signs can suggest an object or idea to another mind. He will picture its form, or mark its height, or imitate its motions, or he may do what he sees others do in connection with it. Thus he snaps his fingers and pats his thigh to signify a dog: he holds an imaginary steering wheel to indicate driving; he puts two fingers astride a third to illustrate horse-riding. He twirls a forefinger in circles and puts a hand to the ear to represent a record player or tape recorder. Or he may suggest an object by imitating its effects; so in suggesting an onion, he pretends to peel it and with many opening and closing of the eyes indicates distress. A person is described by putting a hat on a head and indicating the height of the wearer.

It was argued by exponents of the purely oral system that signing was incapable of conveying abstract ideas, but this is not true: all ideas and emotions have their modes of outward manifestation; and it is by giving free, uninhibited play to motions, attitudes and expressions that feelings are represented by signs. Fear, with alarmed expression, shrinks backwards from the thing of danger. Shame hangs its head. In hatred, the hands are placed upon the heart, and then with open palms push away some imaginary object. Desire extends the hands and works the fingers, as if to take hold of the object sought. Hope places the right hand extended far forward, and the other pointing to it and working as if to reach it as in desire. In pity, the countenance, full of sympathy, looks towards the object of his compassion, and puts out a hand as if tenderly touching it.

One thing that is noticed in sign language is its scanty allusion to time. Even the present tense is not used. But the language is not incapable of expressing time; it can and does express all the tenses whenever required. But unlike verbal language, signing does not repeat the intimation of time with every action. There are many spoken words which are not expressed in signs; for example, there are no conjunctions, such as when and then. The sentence 'After dinner I will go into town' becomes 'Dinner done, town I go.' Non-verbal signals are used in asking questions; the eyebrows are raised as the question is signed, the head tilted forward, shoulders hunched as the final sign is held.

But expressive as they are, these methods can be vague when used in communicating with untrained hearing people, so manual alphabets were eventually devised to use with or without manual sign. This was the only means of communication for the deaf until Heinicke introduced his techniques by which children learn to lip-read what is said to them and taught to speak words they cannot hear. To distinguish it from signing (the French system) Heinicke's 'pure oral' method became known as the German system. The system was further developed by a German teacher, Wilhelm Van Praagh, who held that in teaching by the oral system all signing (including finger-spelling) must be 'rigidly excluded'. Here were the beginnings of the Great Controversy.

But the pure oral method is beset with difficulties and problems. It is difficult to teach and altogether beyond the capabilities of some children; furthermore, it can only be taught in small classes. Efficient lipreading will enable a deaf person to carry on a simple conversation – but only in a clear light. And again, lipreading is largely a matter of guessing since many of the movements of articulation are identical; for example, the mouthing of P, B and M all look exactly alike.

Another difficulty in teaching by the pure oral method is that not only sounds, but many words look alike when spoken on the lips, and the context is not always clear. The great advantage of the combined system is that signs can clarify the natural uncertainty of oralism; for while any sentence is being spoken normally, the appropriate signs are used at the same time. Here are two examples: 'Twenty-six sheep' and 'Twenty sick sheep'. By signing the number 26 or 20, and the word 'sick' or 'six' as the case may be, all ambiguity is avoided. Another is 'while there's life there's hope' which, if not spoken clearly, may be misread orally as 'Where's the lavender soap', but the added use of the signs for 'life' and 'hope' prevents misunderstanding.

Oral training in the form of lip-reading and articulation was used in Britain by the Braidwoods and the Watsons but, because of its difficulties, was supplemented by signing and writing. This combination of methods became known as the combined method, for frequently there are words, especially difficult ones, for which there are no signs. These are spelt out without fear of misunderstanding by use of the manual alphabet.

In the years leading up to 1880, the 'oral *v* signing' controversy developed into a state of open warfare between the advocates of the two systems until a state of conciliation of the two methods was effected. These became known as Pure Oral and Signology. The middle ground or combined systems, seems to have been dropped. This was the situation when over 200 specialists met in Italy to consider this and a number of other pressing and problematic matters concerning deaf education.

9

Long Live Speech

It is not on the deaf-mute's being taught to articulate that his capability to reason depends, but on his being a member of the great family of human beings whose minds are capable of reasoning.

W.R.Scott – *The Deaf and Dumb and Their Education*

In April 1880 Richard Elliott received an invitation to attend the International Congress on the Education of the Deaf to be held later in the year in Milan. He informed his committee of the invitation, but the news was received coldly. He was instructed that if he attended the Congress he would not have the authority to act as an official representative of the Asylum. Then, Edwin Gallaudet (son of Thomas Gallaudet who, in 1815, had applied to train at the Kent Road school), an influential figure in the world of American Deaf education, wrote to the Committee strongly recommending that the school should send someone to Milan on its behalf. As a result, the Committee changed its mind and Elliott was instructed to represent the school at the Congress.

The Milan meeting was attended by over 200 teachers, missioners, doctors and interested lay-people; France and Italy being particularly well represented. The Congress lasted for six days and throughout all the sittings there was an air of great enthusiasm. At the end of the first session, the entire audience was so moved that it rose as a body and shouted '*Evviva la parola*'

– 'Long live speech.'

The discussions and debates that followed cut across all the questions and problems of deaf education that had been the centre of controversy for decades. They included a demand for state aid for deaf education; that education for the deaf child should follow as closely as possible the methods used for normal children; that admission to schools for the deaf should be between the ages of eight and ten; and that ten children were the maximum that one teacher could effectively teach.

But the subject that dominated the Congress was the Great Controversy and, after the opening formalities, work began with a two-day debate on a proposition that begged the very question implied in the controversy:

> State the advantages of the Articulation method over that of signs, or the contrary, regarding it chiefly from an educational point of view, without neglecting its relation to social life.

It was clear from the first day that the general opinion of the delegates was overwhelmingly in favour of the oral system – and not merely 'oral' but what had become known as Pure Oral in which all and any forms of signing were an anathema to be not merely discouraged but abolished. There was then a heated discussion on the difference between 'conventional' and 'natural' signing – the latter being defined as signing which could be understood by deaf and hearing persons alike. Then it was decided that even 'natural signs' could not be tolerated except perhaps that the small deaf child might be allowed a few gestures when first introduced to school life.

It was almost unanimously agreed that wherever signs are permitted, language inevitably suffers, and that 'the sign system' and the 'speech system' cannot exist together. Signing was described as a dialect which set the deaf person apart. The teacher cannot communicate with his class in sign; the deaf cannot link secondary ideas to the principal idea. Signs cannot elicit reasoning, reflection, generalization and, above all, abstraction. The deaf do not perceive their own signs; signs interfere with manual labour. Most of the speakers were passionate in their arguments for the abolition of signing. Let the pupil be taught to move his lips in speech, not his hands. The pure oral method was not only possible but imperative! And so it went on throughout the debate.

The combined, or English method was briefly disposed of as being illogical and impracticable. It was impossible as a teaching method because, it the teacher moves the fingers, arms, head and the whole body at the same time as the lips, the pupil's attention is distracted. A resolution was passed recommending that 'the simultaneous employment of speech and of signs has the disadvantage of injuring speech and lip-reading as well as precision of ideas.' Only a few delegates had anything good to say about the combined method and they were led by Richard Elliott. He presented a paper in which he said 'that experience teaches that the combined system is the best', and he asked that this method should be adopted.

It may be said that the enthusiasm for the pure oral system that dominated the Milan Congress amounted almost to a mania and it is difficult to account for this. The system had been practised since the mid-eighteenth century and was known, even by Heinicke himself, to be suitable only for the instruction of the semi-mute and for the brightest of pupils. It was also known that it produced unnatural-sounding speech and that it tended to slow a child's mental development. Yet at the Congress it was argued that the pure oral system not only teaches speech but permits normal communication, facilitates the acquisition of ideas and restores the deaf to society.

Between the sittings, all delegates were urged to attend exhibitions of the achievements of the oral method that had been arranged at the two local institutions for deaf education. But it seems that the delegates were, to a large extent, being hoodwinked at these sessions. One American delegate reported:

> There was evidence of long previous preparation, of severe drilling. My neighbours, themselves Italian and articulation teachers, informed me that the best pupils were not congenitally deaf and had probably mastered speech before entering the institution.

Another delegate agreed:

> I found that many of the pupils exhibited as illustrating what the pure oral method could accomplish with deaf-mutes had in fact learned to speak before losing their hearing.

Richard Elliott who, it will be remembered, had experienced this kind of deception during his early days at the London Asylum, was not deceived. In a letter from Milan he wrote:

> . . . everything had been carefully rehearsed beforehand . . . (The pupils) did answer correctly, for there were apparently no mistakes made nor was there any deliberation before the answers were given.

He also noticed that the teachers mouthed their words most elaborately and even then were not understood 'when off the beaten track'. He asked to see the children lipread while an Italian stranger read a passage unknown to them. His request was refused. He was later to report that the Congress:

> was mainly a partisan gathering. The machinery to register its decrees on the lines desired by its promoters has evidently been prepared beforehand and to me it seemed that the main feature was enthusiasm and fervidly eloquent advocacy of the 'orale pure' rather than the calm deliberation of the advantages and disadvantages of methods.

But, inevitably, a resolution was passed almost unanimously that the oral method should be preferred to that of signs.

Congress then dealt with the rest of the agenda – class size, age of admission, desirability of teacher training, and so on. On the fourth day Richard Elliott made a powerful speech calling for state aid for deaf education in which he said that the work of benevolent societies was not enough, and that for want of government intervention and help, many deaf children in Britain were growing up with very little education, and many more without any instruction whatever. That to all deaf mutes education was not merely an advantage but a necessity.

The Congress closed after adopting the following chief resolutions.

> That the Pure Oral method is preferred.
> That Governments should take necessary steps that all deaf and dumb children may be educated.
> That deaf children should commence their education at the age of 8.

The most important resolution, which was carried by 116 votes to sixteen, was:

> Considering the incontestable superiority of articulation over signs in restoring the deaf-mute to Society and giving him a fuller knowledge of a language, the Congress declares that the oral method should be preferred to that of signs in the education and instruction of the deaf.

And that:

> The deaf and dumb taught by the Pure Oral Method do not forget after leaving school the knowledge which they have acquired there, but develop it further by conversation and reading, which have been made so

> easy for them.
> That in their conversation with speaking persons they make use exclusively of speech.
> That speech and lipreading, so far from being lost, are developed by practice.

And finally:

> The Congress, considering the incontestable superiority of speech over signs, for restoring deaf-mutes to social life and for giving them greater facility in language, declares that the method· of articultion should have preference over that of signs in the instruction and education of the deaf and dumb.

The resolutions concerning oral v signs are plainly contradictory, for if speech has all the advantages for the deaf and signing all the defects, there would be no need to forbid the use of signs in class and playground; or to segregate older children who sign from those who do not. The deaf themselves would embrace speech as a matter of course.

Nevertheless the oralists were jubilant. One of them, the celebrated French teacher, Abbé Tarra, wrote: 'All discussions have ceased, serious objections (to oralism) have of themselves disappeared, and the long struggle between systems has ended.'

But an American delegate wrote:

> 1880 was the year that saw the birth of the infamous Milan resolution that paved the way for foisting upon the deaf everywhere a loathed method; hypocritical in its claims, unnatural in its application, mind-deadening and soul-killing in its ultimate results.

In time, the victory of pure oralism was to prove short-lived but in many other respects Milan was the turning point in the history of deaf education and welfare. Those who were there realized and proclaimed that notwithstanding the efforts of a century, the deaf child still remained isolated from the normal. The overall conclusions reached by the Congress amounted to a declaration to the world that, save for deafness, the deaf child is normal, and that the way to conserve and extend that normality lay along normal lines of educational procedure and general training – conclusions which Richard Elliott had arrived at long ago. Milan invested him with still more power of authority to carry out his long-term ideas.

10

A New Era: 1880–1899

> *Speech is human, silence is divine, yet also brutish and dead: therefore we must learn both arts.*
>
> **Carlyle**

After Milan the cry of EVVIVA LA PAROLA resounded as the delegates returned home inspired with enthusiasm for a new attitude towards deaf education. A process began whereby the oral method was adopted as the preferred method in all countries except the United States. In Britain most schools adopted it at once, while some wavered for a while; but eventually nearly all became convinced of its superiority.

There is no single explanation for the tide of 'pure oralism' that engulfed Europe, unless it was, as the American historian of deaf education, Harlan Lane, suggests:

> . . . the confluence of nationalism, elitism, commercialism, and family pride. Another contributing cause was the educators' desire for total control of their classrooms, which cannot be had if the pupils sign and the teacher knows none. The teacher becomes a linguistic outcast, the handicapped. There was a time when teachers of the deaf could not practice without a knowledge of their pupils' primary language. But the vast expansion of schools in Europe and America

> created more professional positions than there were educators and administrators fluent in sign. Increasingly, people with few ties to the deaf community dominated their education.
>
> *When the Mind Hears;* Harlan Lane

On returning home the British delegation at once called a meeting of most of the governing bodies of British schools for the deaf to consider the resolutions of what became known as 'the deaf child's Magna Carta.' A deputation from this meeting laid the Milan resolutions before the Government, but were told that nothing could be done at the time; the matter of oral training was of no concern to government, but the schools were free to introduce it if they so wished. But, apart from all the fuss about pure oralism, the British government, and governments all over the world were, as a result of the Conference, eventually to undertake the responsibility of supporting and supervising the education of the deaf, and the subject at last took its recognized place in the world of educational progress.

Meanwhile the oral v signing issue continued. Elliott was but one of a distinguished body of educationalists who at first had found it difficult to believe that there was anything in teaching the oral system worth the time and trouble it involves. He had been a champion of the combined method for years. In a letter to the Journal of the Society of Arts in 1871 he had stated that:

> 'The Combined system, which is the wisest method of instruction, is gaining ground in every country but our own.' And at the conference of teachers of the deaf held in 1877 he had read a paper opposing the adoption of the pure oral system. Then, on his return from the Congress he admitted 'I cannot accept the decisions of the Congress as conclusive.'

But for all his criticism of what he had seen and heard and for all his championing of the combined system in the paper he read to the Congress, he had, if only temporarily, become a convert to pure oralism, for he lost no time in winning the support of the Committee for its introduction at Margate. And yet it seems that he still had reservations, for on this topic we find in Elliott an indecision that, for him, is rare. It seems possible that his temporary switch of allegiance was that he was caught up in the stream of oralism that swept the world of deaf education after Milan. But he never fully adopted the Pure Oral method at Margate; he hovered between it and the Combined systems, whilst always retaining signing for 'backward' children. Some twenty-odd years after the Milan Congress he still seemed unsure of himself, for in 1903 he wrote to the *Teacher of the Deaf:*

> If signing be allowed to grow up instead of language as a medium of intercourse, we shall invariably find the habits of thought and expression are induced which will form a serious obstacle to the acquirement of correct written and spoken language and therefore the work of education generally.

Then later in the same year, and to the same journal, he wrote:

> We may in time arrive at that desirable end, the conciliation of [the two] methods.

And later still, at a Conference of teachers held in Edinburgh in 1907 he observed that 'even poor speech is an asset' and recommended teachers of the deaf 'to give all or the main part of instruction orally'.

Following Milan there are many references to 'oral' in Elliott's reports and those of the Committee, but it is certain that the pure oral regime was never strictly enforced at Margate. A man of Elliott's temperament could not have entirely prohibited the use of signs among his pupils, for he knew that even if it were feasible to do so, such a restriction would force pupils to struggle violently with themselves, thus disturbing, confusing and eventually stopping their intellectual development. Elliott made his position clear at a Conference of Headmasters of deaf education held in 1881. He acknowledged the difficulties of using the oral system with poor teacher/pupil ratio and called for the manual method for those who could not benefit from oralism. 'We shall adopt the system to the pupils,' he said, 'not the pupils to the system.'

In December 1880 the first tentative steps were taken to introduce the pure oral system at Margate with the formation of one oral class and the intention of expanding the system to include almost the entire school. Five years later, Elliott was forced to admit that of the school's total of 318 pupils, only ninety were being instructed in 'pure oral' and that 'the majority are and have been up to the present time under the combined system'.

Before beginning the oral experiment the Committee made a public appeal for funds to make the proposed changes. To this end an advertisement was published in *The Times*. After describing the Asylum and its work the appeal gave details of the proposed changes in teaching methods:

> To inaugurate classes of newly-elected children (to be kept entirely separate from the other children), who shall be taught on the pure oral system, by teachers especially appointed for that purpose.
>
> To extend the education term by one and a half years, admitting children at 7 instead of 8½ years – this extension seems to be a necessity admitted by all teachers of the oral system.
>
> To elect 40 children (a larger number than usual) at the election on the 10th of January next.
>
> To locate those newly-elected children in the Asylum in the Old Kent Road.
>
> To provide specially selected teachers.
>
> To provide a new staff of servants not committed in any way to the use of signs, and thus give the new system a complete and fair trial.

The Committee then advertized for teachers proficient in the oral system, but received no replies – this was because the resolutions of the Milan Congress had created a great demand for teachers with oral experience. The Committee soon discovered that there was also a shortage of teachers suitable for training in the oral method: figures show that of the total of 175 teachers then employed in British deaf institutions, thirty-three were themselves deaf-and-dumb and so incapable of teaching by the oral method. The Committee had no choice but to employ hearing novices and teach them the new system.

A trial period was started at the London branch with thirty-five children, all newly admitted for the purpose of the experiment. The age of entry was altered from the limit of eight and a half to eleven and a half years, which had long prevailed, to the Milan recommendation of seven to ten years. The school in the Old Kent Road was used for oral instruction alone and no signing or finger-spelling was allowed in class. All those who were, or had been, taught by these methods were sent to the newly enlarged school at Margate where the oral, combined and signing systems were all taught in separate classes. Elliott himself trained the new oral teachers with lectures, and formed several classes of advancement. None of the trainee teachers knew any sign or letter of the manual alphabet, and Elliott was careful not to use any and discouraged their acquisition. This continued until the teachers had gained sufficient proficiency to put the method into practice by themselves.

The sytem adopted and maintained for many years was as follows. All new entrants were accommodated at the Old Kent Road to be taught by the oral method for one year, after which they were sent to Margate. The purpose of this was strictly to isolate them from signing until such time as they had a grasp of articulation. On their arrival at Margate their progress and abilities were assessed. Those considered capable of fully mastering articulation continued with the oral system, others progressed to the combined classes, whilst those few children who, for any reason, proved incapable of learning speech were put to signing. Oral classes were in the ratio of about ten pupils per teacher – as recommended by the Milan Congress. The Committee issued a description of the oral methods used at the Old Kent Road:

> The first step is to train in the muscles of the visible vocal organs to act as required for the utterance of definite sounds. After this comes the utterance of sounds, and these should be graded in the order of difficulty of acquirement. Then the characters by which they are known are taught, and constant exercises are given to develop of utterance of the sounds, and to enable them to be put together with readiness. During this process a considerable number of words may be learned. The peculiarities of utterances are also recognized by the pupil, and become his means of identifying them, so that from lip-reading of sounds, he may in the next stage get to lip-reading of words. This portion – the gaining of the mechanism of speech – has taken about one year.
>
> The teacher's object is to get the children to learn as far as possible like hearing children. Having given them the power to utter definite sounds, and to imitate them by their visible peculiarities, it is possible to build up words by combining such sounds, and for the pupil at this stage to *say* words. But of course their *meaning* lies quite apart from mere utterance. The next point is to give the pupils so much of the ordinary spoken language as will enable one to converse with them on simple topics. This will all have to be gone through before education proper can be commenced. And this colloquial language, which is the grand stumbling block of those taught by signs, is the 'Pure Oral' system to stand in lieu of signs.

On this report, Richard Elliott commented:

> There is one point, which I must confess is somewhat of a surprise to me. It is that the children (taught by the oral system) . . . sign to each other in natural signs out of school. To forbid this would be cruel to them, and almost impossible to carry out. But there is an absence of signs in the schoolroom and the attempt is made to lead the children to discard signs altogether in favour of the more effectual and educational medium of communication, speech.
>
> (School Minute Books 1860)

George Woodford, a pupil at Margate at this time remembers being 'rapped over the knuckles' for using signs, although he disliked signing and used finger-spelling; but nevertheless, he learned to write immaculate English. A journalist visiting the Old Kent Road Asylum at this time wrote his impressions for the *Saturday Journal*:

> Conversation by means of signs is discountenanced, oral language being now deemed sufficient. The children however, have made up a code of signals of their own, and it is impossible to prevent them from using it, as it is in many cases the only method of communicating ideas that they possess.
>
> In the classroom an eight-year-old girl is having an 'oral lesson':
>
> The instructress takes her hand, and places it against her own throat, so that the child may hear the vibrations of her voice. She then loudly utters the sound 'Ah!'
>
> The child, of course, can hear nothing; she is stone deaf. But she can feel the vibrations of the teacher's throat, and she can see the form taken by her lips. The child's hand and throat are now placed in contact, and

> her mouth is opened wide by her instructress. The poor little thing tries to imitate her mistress, but her efforts at first result in nothing more than a forcible expulsion of breath. Again and again she tries in the same way, till after several failures tears begin to gather in her eyes. At last she succeeds in producing a very slight and uncertain sound – her first step towards the acquisition of language.

Thirty-nine children entered the Margate school in 1882, twenty-nine of them from the Old Kent road. Four, having been taught signing by deaf relatives at their homes, could not cope with the change and were put in the signing class. Another four joined them as being considered incapable of oral teaching. The remainder were put to oral instruction.

The results of Elliott's experiments in oral training reflected those in other schools in the country. The great expectations expressed so enthusiastically at Milan did not materialize and in the event the great oral revolution came to nothing. In the light of today's knowledge, it is not unfair to say that those assembled at Milan had no adequate conception either of the natural physiology of speech and language, or of the psychology of the deaf child. This is evident from their limitation of the use of language to speech ability; and the declaration that the best age to begin teaching the deaf is eight years. Hodgson says that this was the 'least happy' of the Milan resolutions, a matter of mistaken kindness and part of:

> that general nineteenth-century maternalism which wanted to shield the afflicted from hardship. It was and is a crime to wrench very young deaf children away from home to immure them in a barrack-like boarding-school. But the remedy lay not in handicapping the children to fit the schools, but in altering the schools to suit younger children.
>
> (Hodgson *op. cit.*)

Richard Elliott was well aware of the problem of 'barrack-like' surroundings and on his return from Milan he continued his efforts to improve the living conditions and atmosphere of the school. In 1882, he presented a report to the Committee which recommended that:

> The Institution should be divested of the still angularity of a barrack-like life, and should be as much as possible a home for both pupils and teachers. The future life of the former with their grievous deprivation must be a hard one at best; it should be our task to make their school life a bright and happy one, to which they may always look back with pleasure. For the latter, a home will attach them to the work, and retain, for the important task they have to do, their experience and skill which will enable them to do it effectually. The work requires much to brighten it; for it is often monotonous, frequently discouraging, and always demands more than ordinary patience, self-denial and kindliness.

With the Committee's backing, he put some of his ideas into effect. He further modified and relaxed the disciplinary system, whereby in some cases requiring punishment he ordered the offenders to spend the day wearing their coats back-to-front; this was found to be quite as effective as corporal punishment. He also established the school's first library and had success in fostering the reading habit amongst his charges. He arranged that whenever possible children should be sent to friends during the summer holiday so that they could gain some experience of the world they would enter when their school days were over. He also endeavoured that the children should be allowed to go out alone for walks or errands, but the Committee objected to this as dangerous – although Elliott got his way in the end. In the meantime he himself took parties of children on railway trips to neighbouring towns. But boys and girls were still segregated with two divisions being maintained in class and even in church, where, during services, a lively communication was maintained between the sexes by the passing of notes. This Victorian segregation continued well into the 1950s.

The Old Kent Road premises had long been in need of extensive renovation, and in 1885 the Committee decided 'not to put the building in complete repair' but instead to close it permanently and 'give the orally trained children there the benefit of a seaside home'. Richard Elliott was instructed to find a suitable building for the purpose in or near Margate and to transfer to it the fifty orally-trained children remaining at the Old Kent Road. This was only a temporary move to allow Elliott the convenience of superintending both branches of the school until such time as the Margate school could be enlarged to accommodate all the children under one roof. He eventually found Cavendish House, a large building at St Lawrence in Ramsgate. This was rented, and in January 1886 the London children were transferred there to continue their education in isolation from the combined and silently taught children. The school in the Old Kent Road was then closed and demolished. Nevertheless, the Committee 'not wishing to be disassociated entirely from the Old Kent Road' retained a presence on the site by building a small school where fifty newly received children were to receive one year's training before going to Margate. The new building was occupied in April 1887.

In the process of introducing the oral method, the size of classes at Margate had been much reduced. By 1885 there were twenty children in each of the seven sign and finger-spelling classes, whilst the oral and combined taught children were in seventeen classes of about ten in each. With the memory of Milan in mind, the Committee had held to their aim of making the school purely oral, but by 1886 the many drawbacks to the system had become apparent and the Committee was having second thoughts. In a report of that year it stated:

It is now five years since they (the Committee) first

made the attempt at teaching the oral system, and had now 90 children who were being taught on that system. When they came to consider the education of deaf children it was very important that they should not lose sight of different physical capacities, which were very various, and in many cases stunted, by the surroundings in which they lived in the earliest years. Last year several members of the Committee visited a school on the oral system in Yorkshire, and they were struck with the intelligence of the children.

When they came to enquire they found that they were children of artisans, engineers, and people working in the factories, people whose wits were sharpened, and the sharpness spread itself to the intelligence of the children. But let them (the Committee) recollect that the children in their schools came from the lowest strata of poverty. Almost all the children came from very poor and in many cases very unhappy localities, and hardly any of the parents had the capacity to give their deaf children anything like an early education.

The whole matter having been looked into for five years, the Committee have come to the unanimous conclusion that so far as possible the oral system of teaching should be the one adopted. Those not capable of receiving instruction orally will still be taught, and taught well, by the silent system.

Further expansion of the Margate school took place in 1886 with the building of a new wing. There was also a first-aid room and an infirmary standing separately from the main building. Sporting facilities were also enlarged with a football field and a hockey pitch. External fire escapes were constructed and a direct telegraph line was laid to the local fire-station. To meet recent legislation on cubic feet per child, the Committee decided to limit the numbers to 180 boys and 140 girls.

Progress in deaf and blind education continued throughout

the rest of the nineteenth century. In 1884 a Committee of five teachers was appointed by the Royal Association in Aid of the Deaf and Dumb to arrange for the training of teachers of the deaf and to award certificates of proficiency. This pioneering committee was led by Elliott and Stainer, and from it was formed the College of Teachers of the Deaf and Dumb which opened in July 1885 in Stainer House in Paddington. The objects of the college were to 'disseminate knowledge' concerning deaf education, to promote activity for the general welfare of the deaf, and to improve standards of teaching by awarding diplomas of efficiency. Until that time teachers of the deaf had been an isolated class with no acknowledged position. The provision of diplomas gave them a recognized status for the first time.

In 1885 there was further progress when a Royal Commission was appointed to investigate into the needs and conditions of the blind and the deaf. It was concerned mainly with the blind but was described at the time as 'the most thorough and searching examination the world has ever seen on the problems of the deaf.' The Commission sat from December 1885 to July 1888 and put 22,298 questions to 157 witnesses. Among them was Richard Elliott whose evidence records details of conditions at Margate at the time. There were 318 pupils and twenty-six teachers – twelve male, ten female – and four pupil teachers 'mostly educated at the Asylum'; only one of the teachers (himself an ex-pupil) was deaf.

Elliott's evidence also records that the pure oral policy at Old Kent Road and Margate had been short lived.

> Q: Do you use the oral system exclusively?
> A: Not exclusively.
> Q: To what extent do you not use it?
> A: We are rather peculiarly situated in regard to that. The committee has come to the conclusion that the oral system is the system which should be adopted in the case of as many as can be best taught by it; but that

> conclusion was only arrived at about six months ago. Consequently the majority of the children are and have been up to the present time under the combined system. We have 90 children who have been for more than five years past exclusively under oral teaching.

Elliott also admitted that it was impossible to prevent the oral children from signing when they were out of the classroom; that they 'apply them without any education in signs.'

On the subject of state aid for deaf education, Elliott said:

> As a private opinion I believe that there is no other way of meeting the difficulty of making a full provision for deaf mute education; but speaking as an official connected with the asylum we do not want State aid ourselves.

Elliott said the school did not want state aid because: 'State aid would necessarily involve State interference' and that 'even if a subsidy was forced on the school, it just did not have the room to take more children.' Also it transpired that the Asylum was not in any particular need of extra income at the time, for it owned property worth £159,000 and had a regular income of nearly £9,000 per annum. This was made up of:

Subscriptions	£2,029
Donations	£239
Dividends	£5,000
Rents	£1,700

In addition there was income from collections after special sermons, annuities, payments from paying children, and a grant from the Science and Industry Department. The average cost of keeping and teaching each child was put at £34 per annum.

The evidence and reports of the Commission were published in 1889 as a Blue Book of four volumes containing 1574 pages.

The chief recommendations were:

> that the provisions of the Education Acts should be extended to the Deaf and Dumb;
> that attendance of children should be compulsory between the ages of seven and sixteen years;
> that technical training in industrial skills should be given;
> that every child should have full opportunity of being educated on the pure oral system;
> that 'less intelligent' children could be taught by other methods, but segregated from other pupils.
> that a training college for teachers of the deaf should be established.
> that the terms of deaf-mute, and deaf and dumb should not be used unless appropriate.
> that trained teachers should have higher salaries than those of teachers of normal children;
> that inspectors of schools for the deaf should be experts in the subject.

Apart from the recommendation concerning the pure oral system, all these proposals had been advocated by Richard Elliott for years. But there the matter rested, for it took another four years fully to incorporate the recommendations into an Act of Parliament. In the meantime the school commemorated its centenary year with treats, celebrations and other events – which included the building of a workshop for 'hand and eye' training. It was estimated that during its one hundred years the school had received and educated over 5,000 children of whom over 2,000 had been successfully apprenticed to trades and other callings.

In 1893 the recommendations of the 1886 Commission were at long last incorporated in the Elementary Education (Blind and Deaf Children) Act which included the first granting of direct government aid to deaf children.

For years many charities had opposed state aid for their work – some had even resisted the Poor Law Act of 1845 which, amongst other measures, authorized Boards of Guardians to assist in the instruction of the deaf and dumb. Even this was seen as 'state aid' and therefore a breach of the Victorian principle of *laissez faire*. One Dr Scott of the West of England Institution commented:

> In a country where unlimited competition so thoroughly educates the selfish element of our nature, some compensating opposite principle is necessary for the moral life of our society.

In other words; God puts the disabled and disadvantaged on earth as a chance for the rich and selfish to salve their consciences! Furthermore, official funding of every sort was disapproved of by those who believed that private charity provided an insight and an education to the giver of the needs of the disadvantaged.

Among other measures the Elementary Education Act of 1893 required the compulsory attendance of deaf children at schools and laid down that every school authority must provide efficient and suitable education for them in a certified school in their district. The local authorities were also required to contribute to the establishment or upkeep of at least one certified school and to arrange for the boarding out of any deaf child under their care who attended such a school. Inspectors from the Education Department would inspect schools which, if certified, would receive a grant of three guineas per head per year for general studies – ie reading, writing, etc and two guineas for vocational training such as carpentry and needlework. The money for this purpose was to come from central funds. Also, for the first time, local school authorities, as opposed to Guardians, were empowered to pay for the maintenance of deaf children whose parents, because of poverty, were unable to support them.

Private schools were not covered by this legislation. Furthermore there was a proviso which required that when a school was not managed by a School Authority, at least one third of its annual expenses of maintaining the school should be derived from private (ie charitable) sources. One of the results of the 1893 Act was the growth of many day schools, so that by 1939, some 4,000 children were being educated in schools for the deaf in the UK.

The Act's provisions for the deaf were meagre, and it may be suspected that they were not entirely charitable, but directed to training the deaf to make them self-sufficient rather than a burden on the rates. But they did amount to the recognition of the right of deaf children to publicly-funded education. That deaf children could at last attend school by right represented a victory for Richard Elliott and his fellow workers.

The only immediate effect of the Act on the school was that it made education compulsory for deaf children between the ages of seven and sixteen. School-leaving age at Margate was then ten years, so a certain amount of squeezing had to be done. The problem was solved by rearranging the new school in London to keep children there for an additional six months, thus to relieve the pressure at Margate. Otherwise the school disregarded the Act. It did not want state interference – or, for that matter, state money, so it remained a strictly charitable institution. The Committee even declined to be represented at a conference of teachers of the deaf called to discuss the implications of the Act on the ground that they had no intention of registering the school under the Act's provisions.

When, in 1896, the Rev. J.W.Gedge, the school inspector made his usual annual examination of the Margate children (for the twenty-first successive year) he was able to comment:

> On my first visit in 1875 the children were massed in large classes, with no regular system. The teachers were hardly trained at all. The schoolroom was noisy

> and inconvenient and [separate] class rooms almost unknown.
>
> There were not two children who could produce an intelligible articulate sound.
>
> In contrast, what is there now? A good preparatory school in London; a noble building at Margate; teachers thoroughly trained and competent; a definite and progressive course of instruction; a higher point of education than was ever dreamt of twenty years ago.

His report said that practically every child leaving the school could read and understand the lips of anyone who troubled to speak slowly; that the 'oral children', on leaving, could speak clearly enough to be understood in the outside world; that the language of the elder children was equal to 'seventh standard' children in normal elementary schools, while their accuracy and beautiful writing was superior; and that they could calculate money and make out bills as neatly and as accurately as an ordinary boy clerk.

In 1899 Elliott made another of his regular tours of UK schools for the deaf. In reporting to the Committee on this exercise he took the opportunity of pressing for another improvement in conditions at Margate:

> In comparison with every other institution for the deaf, our girls are far too heavily worked in the domestic department. If their parents realized what they are required to do there would be great dissatisfaction. In a letter to me, Mrs Story one of our most valued teachers, speaks of how the first-class girls come into school in the morning 'completely tired out' after two hours 'hard scrubbing,' and that their attendance in school is merely 'a rest' – hard intellectual work being an impossibility. It would not be so bad if the work being done had any educational value, either as housework or laundry-work. On the contrary, it seems

> to be mainly, or entirely, the performance of the dirty work, the drudgery, in relief of the domestics. A late matron used to say that the employment of children spoilt her servants. The universal testimony is that where deaf girls are associated in the kitchen or laundry-work they are hard put upon and made drudges. Our girls are so obedient, so willing, and so industrious that they have rarely complained. Their lot in life must often be a very sad one, when they leave us, and I am sure it must be your wish that the period of their youth should have all the brightness that can be brought into it. I therefore venture to suggest on their behalf, that you put them on an equal footing with girls of other institutions for the deaf, by withdrawing them from the scrubbing, and the kitchen and laundry-work, especially when it is done in school hours. This proposal may mean the addition of a servant to the domestic staff, but even if so, the benefit will be cheaply purchased.

Elliott's determination on matters affecting the children's welfare was such that there can be little doubt that this recommendation was soon put into effect.

11

The Royal School: 1901–1923

'Train up a child in the way he should go; and when he is old, he will not depart from it.'
Proverbs XXII,6

For the Asylum for the Deaf and Dumb Children of the Poor, the twentieth century began with the death of its royal patron, Queen Victoria. The Committee sent a letter of sympathy to the new King, Edward VII with the request that he continue the patronage. His agreement to this request was recorded in the year's Annual Report:

> The Committee have the pleasure to announce that His Majesty, who has been, as Prince of Wales, for so many years the Patron of the Institution, has graciously consented to retain his position, and as an additional mark of his favour has granted the use of the title 'Royal'. The Committee have allocated 30 additional votes to His Majesty as Patron, making 50 votes in all. The Committee wish to inform their supporters and subscribers and all whom it may concern that the correct title of the Institution, in accordance with the Act of Incorporation, is 'Royal Asylum for the Deaf and Dumb Poor', and not 'Asylum for the Education of the Deaf and Dumb Children of the Poor'.

When the continuation of royal support had been secured, a flagstaff was erected in the grounds of the Margate school. It bears the following inscription:

> This flagstaff, the cost of which was defrayed by the contributions of the present and past pupils of the Asylum and their friends, was erected in the first year of the reign of His Majesty, King Edward VII in commemoration of his accession to the throne and in acknowledgement of his gracious consent to continue as Patron of this Asylum and also in testimony of the sincere attachment of the pupils to their School.

By 1900 all but eighty of the 300 Margate children were being trained by the combined method in classes of about a dozen, and the results more than justified Elliott's faith in the method. A visitor to the school at this time reported that:

> Some of the results are remarkable. Several children to whom I spoke understood what I said without apparent difficulty, and some had voices so pleasant that I wondered whether, if they had been blessed with the organ of sound, they would not have made the most excellent singers.

One profoundly deaf pupil of this time was destined to make his name as a Royal Academician and painter of royal portraits. His name was Alfred Reginald Thomson and he was admitted in January 1901 at the age of seven. His promise as an artist was recognized when he was 11 and he was promoted to the top of the art class. In 1909 his family decided to transfer him to a private school for the deaf in Brondesbury, London. His father wrote the following letter to the secretary of the Royal School:

> My son, as you are aware, has shown some talent for drawing and painting, and I have decided to give him

a thorough art training which he will have better opportunities of getting in London than in the Provinces. If not for this, I would prefer him to remain at Margate, where he has made such excellent progress. I am very much indebted to the Institution for the very great kindness shown to him and for the special pains taken in his case, and I am sure that he will always look back with gratitude to the excellent training he has received there from sympathetic and skilful teachers. Any success he may achieve in after life will be due to the healthy influences which operate at Margate. Whenever I visited Margate I have always been struck by the cheerful and happy spirit prevailing among the children, both in and out of the school. This is indeed a great feature of the system followed, which brings such a happy tone into the home life of the children; that instead of growing up shy and morbid, the children are always bright and happy and thoroughly interested in all, that goes on around them.

My son has always shown his readiness to return to the school after the holidays, an indication of the kindness which he has experienced, and I am certain that he will consider the years he has spent in Margate as some of the happiest of his life.

Pray convey my heartiest thanks to the Headmaster, teachers and Matron of the Institution for all they have done for him.*

In 1902, George, Prince of Wales, invited a party of sixty Margate children to view the coronation procession of his father, Edward VII, from the grounds of Marlborough House on June 26, the proposed day of the coronation. In the event the ceremony had to be postponed owing to the King's illness, but the children's visit to Marlborough House took place on the day

---

Tommy A Biography of the distinguished deaf royal painter, A. R. Thomson, R.A., R.P., R.B.A., (1894–1979) by Arthur F. Dimmock (1991).

arranged where they were royally entertained and each presented with a coronation mug.

During the same year the long postponed decision was made finally to close the Old Kent Road school. To provide for this, a new wing was built at Margate consisting of fourteen classrooms, two dormitories, playrooms, a nursery and additional accommodation for teachers. On its completion all the London children were transferred to Margate and the Old Kent Road building was sold to the London School Board for £16,750. After 110 years of pioneering progress in the education of deaf children the old London Asylum ceased to exist. During that time educational and social attitudes to the scourge of deafness had changed beyond recognition. When the school was founded there was only one other in the United Kingdom. That was Braidwood's Academy which was for deaf children of the wealthy. By 1900 3,750 children were attending or living in special schools for the deaf.

The living and teaching conditions that had so appalled Richard Elliott on his arrival in 1857 had been transformed. The workhouse atmosphere, the ill-treatment, the nepotism and the inefficient teaching methods were gone – together with the untrained, underpaid, overworked teachers. The unified school that opened in Margate in 1902 was staffed by qualified, committed people giving systemized instruction in comfortable well-run premises. The Asylum was no longer an asylum. The change was emphasized in 1908 when the words 'Asylum' and 'Poor' with all their old depressing associations were dropped and Margate became the Royal School for Deaf Children.

This change of name seems to signify the change of attitude to the handicapped which continued throughout the present century. It was also a forerunner of the many changes that were about to take place in the school.

In 1905 the school applied for certification under the Elementary Education Act of 1893. The main reason for taking this long-avoided step was the urgent need for additional income due to a falling off of contributions and legacies.

Another reason was that the establishment of schools for the deaf by the London County Council and other borough and county councils, had resulted in a diminishing number of applications for admissions to Margate. In 1898 there had been 345 children on the establishment; by 1904 there were only 290, and the number of candidates for election was falling off year by year. With certification the Royal School would receive children from various Education Authorities.

The school submitted to inspection by a government inspector and was duly granted its certificate. The inspector reported that 'with regard to space and health' no structural or other alterations were required. The report also testified to the efficiency of the school and to the 'just and impartial way in which examinations were conducted.'

On receiving the certificate the Committee sent a circular letter to all the Educational Committees in England:

> . . . The Board of Education having issued a Certificate under the Elementary Education (Blind and Deaf Children) Act, 1893, the Committee of this Institution are now prepared to receive children, as vacancies may occur, on the nomination of the various Educational Authorities in the Kingdom.
>
> The cost of maintenance, clothing and education is £30 per annum. This charge covers the whole year.

The year 1907 marked Richard Elliott's fiftieth anniversary as a teacher at the school, and to mark the occasion the children presented him with an address:

> Sir,
>
> We, the Children of the Margate Asylum, desire to offer our sincerest greetings to you, on this anniversary, for we remember that for just 50 years you have been the Friend of Deaf Children firstly, as a Teacher at the Old Kent Road, and afterwards as Headmaster

in London and Margate.

Many deaf boys and girls have left our school in 50 years – and are now grown-up men and women – in many different places, but all know how kind and good you were to them at school; and we are sure that they would wish us to remember you in this Jubilee year.

We hope that you will continue to have very good health and be with us for many years to come. Also that the future years will be full of happiness for you.

But Elliott did not, as the children hoped, long remain at the school, for in the following year he retired after fifty-one years of continuous service. When he first arrived at the Kent Road establishment, the teaching of speech to poor children hardly existed and lip-reading was non-existent. It was he who, without training or outside help, introduced the oral and combined systems and trained his teachers in them. At the time of his resignation, the great majority of children at Margate were learning to speak, and after-care enquiries showed that most of the 3,000 ex-pupils who had had educational contact with him were using speech in communicating with their employers, relatives and friends.

Elliott's success with the combined method was confirmed in the year of his retirement by the government inspector's report on the school. Of the 332 pupils then in residence, only sixty were in the 'silent classes' – and these were described as 'very backward'. The report contained nothing but praise for the running and living conditions generally. The food was 'ample and nutritious' and the children healthy and free of the 'ailments of children in institutions'. The Inspector also praised the teachers' pension scheme – an innovation in those days – and recommended it to 'other governing bodies in similar circumstances'.

Richard Elliott was succeeded as headmaster by Josh White, head of an LCC residential school for deaf boys in Annerly, south London, and a specialist in manual instruction and trade training for deaf children. His first move was to reorganize the school into Primary, Intermediate and Senior Departments. Over the following years he was instrumental in the building of a technical workshops block where he introduced training in cabinet-making, boot-making and french-polishing for boys. Most of the girls continued to learn laundering, garment-making and housewifery. Separate rooms were set apart for 'advanced' housekeeping classes, where the girls of fifteen to sixteen years of age lived for their last year of school life. They were provided with model shops to learn the techniques of shopping; then, when proficient, were given money to shop in the town for food. They cooked their meals, kept accounts and generally ran households of their own.

White was much concerned in giving all pupils a broad training in the minor, but essential skills of everyday living. To this end he introduced the school's Certificate for General Usefulness which was awarded to boys and girls after a course of general training taken in addition to the special trade.

Girl's Qualifications.

Cut out and make undergarment. Patch a garment. Use the sewing machine. Take measurements. Refoot a sock. Darn a sock. Wash and iron an undergarment and an apron. Clean the kitchen floor and range and flues. Lay a fire. Cook a joint, potatoes and vegetables. Make soup, 3 kinds of pudding. Cook eggs in three different ways. Set a table for dinner and teas. Make a bed and turn out bedroom. Dress an infant. Bandage a finger. Go errands. Give and receive correct change. Swim a distance.

Boy's Qualifications.

Sole and heel own boots. Sew on a patch by hand. Repair trouser bottoms and coat cuffs. Darn socks.

> Take measurements. Plane up a piece of wood true. Grind and sharpen a knife. Put in a pane of glass. Make a picture frame. Fix a hinge and a lock. Repair a sash-cord. Strop a razor. Dig a plot of ground. Go errands. Give and receive correct change. Swim a distance.

On the death of King Edward VII in 1910, King George V and Queen Mary became patrons of the school and during the same year, (for a reason unrecorded), the word 'dumb' was reintroduced to the school's name so that it again became the Royal School for Deaf and Dumb Children.

The 1914–18 war was a time of considerable anxiety for the Committee and the staff, for the school was situated in a dangerous zone. Following air attacks on the south-east coast, an air-raid shelter was built in the school grounds to accommodate 600 people, and the children were drilled to be under cover within minutes of an air-raid warning. Many raids were experienced from both bombers and Zeppelins and there were several bombardments from the sea. A total of twelve bombs exploded in the school grounds but they caused only minor damage to the buildings. There were no injuries to the children or staff – although three of the school's masters were killed on active service.

The Royal School did its share of war work. In the school workshops the girls worked at making a whole range of clothing items for the services, while the senior boys learned Red Cross work – presumably in anticipation of joining up. In 1916 a house in the grounds was furnished and equipped as a small residential school and presented to the government for teaching lip-reading to some of the many hundreds of soldiers rendered deaf during battle. Over one hundred men received free training from the school teaching staff.

In 1915 a follow-up survey was made of the after-school progress of the 290 pupils who had left the school during the six years of White's headmastership. The results showed the effectiveness of his concentration on industrial training. Of the

254 who were capable of working only two were reported as unemployed.

BOYS

Bootmakers	61	Labourers	1
Tailors	26	Munition workers	1
Garden/Farm workers	23	Harness workers	1
Woodworkers	18	Independent means	1
Compositors	8	In Asylums	4
Upholsterers	3	Invalids	2
Engravers	2	Lost trace of	8
Basketmakers	2	Capable/unemployed	1
Brushmakers	2		
Dental mechanics	2		
Packers	1		
Ostlers	1		

GIRLS

Dressmakers	45	Hosiery makers	1
Tailoresses	8	Incandescent Mantle makers	3
Laundresses	27	Married	2
Domestic servants	10	At home	5
Cap makers	1	Invalids	4
Weavers	1	Lost trace of	7
Box makers	2	Capable/unemployed	2
Packers	1		
Milliners	1		
Corset makers	1		

The 1915 follow-up survey showing employment figures.

Eighty-four of those in skilled employment of various kinds were earning between 13s to 45s a week; sixty-five earning between 8s and 12s; and ninety-seven, mostly in apprenticeship, had wages of under 8s a week. The remainder were in 'precarious employment'.

Although the majority of pupils at this time were paid for by local education authorities, there were still a number of free places which were awarded by the old election system. This had remained much the same since 1792, with the entries being decided by the votes of the subscribers. Votes for a single election could be purchased at the rate of four for a guinea; one vote at each election cost five guineas; or an annual subscription of 10s 6d and a subscriber of 200 guineas had forty votes at each half-yearly election, or could keep one child always at the school.

In 1915 twenty children stood as 'candidates', four of whom, two boys and two girls, were elected. The report of the election says: 'The votes for Unsuccessful Candidates will be carried to their credit at the next Election.' It was not until 1927 that the election system was dropped; then each application for entry, whether private of from a local authority, was considered on an individual basis.

No progress in deaf education took place during the years of war. Then, in 1918, came the foundation of the National College of Teachers of the Deaf. This was the result of an amalgamation of the College of Teachers of the Deaf and Dumb (founded in 1885) and the National Association of Teachers of the Deaf which Richard Elliott had been instrumental in forming in 1895. In 1919 Manchester University founded a Department of Education for the Deaf which offered a three-year degree course in the subject – the first university to do so. This professional recognition of teachers of the deaf was the fulfilment of one of Richard Elliott's greatest aims, and it is fitting that he lived to see it.

Also in 1919 there was a change in the system of state aid for the education of blind and deaf children, and the entire cost of their education and maintenance in residential schools was put onto local school authorities. The direct government grant system was discontinued – except in the case of children sent to school by a Board of Guardians; in which case the sum was deducted from the sum paid by the school authorities.

The 1920s was a decade of slow yet steady progress at Margate. In 1920, the Allen Homes were instituted on twenty acres of ground purchased by the school at nearby Park Crescent Road. Here, two small houses were built for the accommodation of twenty young deaf children aged between four and a half and eight who lived under the supervision of specially trained house mothers. These homes were named after Colonel G.J. Allen, a tireless worker for the school who had joined the Committee in 1898. The Allen Homes were enlarged over the following three years until they accommodated sixty-five children of up to eight years old.

In 1923 Richard Elliott died at the age of eighty-seven. Entirely self taught in the art of teaching deaf children, either orally or by signs, he began his career at a time when men like him were urgently needed. Records show that his normal working day was from seven o'clock in the morning until eight o'clock at night, and in addition to the long hours of hard work he spent in the school, he put much of his spare time in writing and lecturing at conferences. His daily journals have survived. They are recorded in detail logging not only the day-by-day life of the school, but recording his deep concern for the children, both collectively and as individuals. Thousands of deaf children passed under his influence and he maintained a keen interest in their after-school life. His record is a grand one. He was loved by his teachers – particularly for his tolerance and justice – and when he died there were teachers all over Britain and the rest of the world who had learned their skills from him.

He was the author of three books on deaf education; *Elementary Lessons in Written Language for the Deaf* (1878), *Articulation and Lip-Reading* (1895) and *Questions of Common Subjects* (1905). These books were among the first in English to reduce the teaching of language to the deaf to a public property, generally available to all teachers of the deaf, and they made it possible for graded instruction in language to become part of the curriculum in deaf schools. Elliott was nationally and internationally acclaimed and in 1891 was awarded the American degree of Doctorate of Humane Letters.

One of Elliott's greatest qualities was his stoical self-control – for without it he could not have accomplished what he did. From the time of his arrival at the Old Kent Road until his appointment as headmaster at Margate he had to accept and cope with the open dislike and enmity of James Watson and the suspicion and lack of cooperation of the Committee. Yet throughout this period of constant provocation he managed to keep his equanimity – and with it his job.

12

Expanding and Modernizing: 1924–1938

Sometimes people say to me, 'What a shame you are deaf.' It makes me so angry. All people are the same, but only I cannot hear. They are just stupid. But the people who are handicapped are worse than me. I just can't hear.

Karen Pinkham, a profoundly deaf Margate pupil 1984

The years 1924–26 were a period of continual rebuilding and improvement. Gas light was replaced by electricity and an artesian well sunk in the grounds. Another technical block for trade training was added, and part of the gymnasium was converted into a cinema for education and entertainment. A small hospital was built for mastoid and other ear operations and in 1925 a swimming pool, with a filtering plant, showers and dressing rooms. On a stretch of land adjoining the school, an 'Instructional Farm' was started in 1926. This was a self-contained unit with cattle, pigs and poultry and had up-to-date facilities for training in the manufacture of dairy products, the preparation of milk for distribution, bacon-curing and smoking and the grading and packing of eggs.

In July 1925 an International Conference on the Education of the Deaf was held in London attended by 350 delegates from all over the world. When it was over a large party of the delegates spent a day touring the Royal School 'to enable them to inspect the oldest Institution for the Deaf in the British Isles and return to their work with the deaf all over the world, with a new standard of comparison.' The day chosen for the visit was for the school's summer fête and was marked by a spectacular portrayal in pageantry of *The Bohemian Girl* in which 250 pupils took part. These pageants became a regular feature of the school's annual fete and were for many years one of the great days in Margate's social calendar.

In 1932, Josh White retired after twenty-four years as headmaster. During his time White was responsible for many changes which brought great benefit to the school as a whole. New departments were founded, including the Allen Nursery Homes and a hostel for older boys in the town. White introduced an art-school with a fully-qualified art teacher and was instrumental in the appointed of an aural surgeon and a bacteriologist to the medical staff. He was known to be sympathetic to parents and sensitive to their needs. He gave them the freedom to visit their children at any time, and also allowed the older pupils to visit the town without supervision. Josh White was succeeded by Alfred (Bill) Swayne, head of the Leeds School for Blind and Deaf Children.

By this time the school accommodated 470 pupils and forty-three teachers, yet despite its thirty acres and all the new building, more room space was needed. In 1933 another block was designed to house eight more classroons and a large gymnasium. These operations were completed in 1935. Also at this time, two hard tennis courts were laid out and a sports pavilion erected by the cricket field. In the cinema, sound equipment was installed with special wiring arrangements which allowed the majority of the children to hear the sound-track through earphones. For the children this was an exciting innovation for electronic hearing-aid equipment had only recently been introduced at the school.

It was not until well into the twentieth century that the physical sciences helped in any significant way the problems of the deaf. Earlier diagnosis of defective hearing and scientific improvements in instruments for testing hearing revealed the fact that in most cases far more 'residual' hearing remained in the deaf individual than had been suspected in the past. Then the development of electronics made it possible to exploit this residual hearing.

Accoustical 'deaf aids' (as they were originally known) were in use throughout the nineteenth century, and were being made by one manufacturer as early as 1800, but there is no evidence of their use at the Royal School until about 1885 when an instrument known as the 'audiphone' was acquired. Nothing came from this experiment except the comment that 'The only use of the audiophone is to those who sell it'. The school had more success in 1889 when it purchased a 'macrophone'. This was, in Elliott's words:

> ... a kind of stethoscope, kindly adapted to our requirements and called a 'macrophone', which seems to answer the purpose intended, and helps materially in the acquirement of spoken sounds.

There is no further reference to the macrophone in the school's records so it must be presumed that its benefits were limited.

In 1890, the aurist, James Kerr Love, made the important discovery that total deafness was rare. Of those he tested, less than ten per cent were totally deaf and twenty-five per cent could understand loud speech. This discovery resulted in considerable excitement in schools for the deaf and much re-appraisal of the benefits of hearing aids. In 1895 the medical officer at Margate, Bernard Thornton, invented and patented a tele-transmitter and earphone powered by three dry-cell batteries which enabled speech reading to take place and which several children could use if the number of earphones was increased. This was the start of teaching with hearing aids at Margate.

The advent and development of electrical amplification in hearing aids began in the 1920s and resulted in research into the problem of finding the most suitable hearing-aid for the individual concerned. In 1926 the audiometer was developed for testing hearing. One type of audiometer used recordings of speech at controlled volume, with multiple ear-phones, so that a whole classroom of children could be tested at the same time.

At the Royal School the subject of hearing-aids was treated with care and caution. They became a matter for discussion for many years and there was considerable difference of opinion on their value amongst the teaching staff. It was not until 1933, following years of research and testing, that an audiometer and the first hearing-aids were purchased.

Initially much difficulty was experienced in the fitting of correct aids for particular types of deafness. Then, after further discussion and experiment, it was decided that partial deafness could be divided into three groups. The first needed amplification of sound only; the second needed compensation for high notes and the third needed compensation for low notes.

An experimental hearing-aid class was formed where it was found that fifteen semi-deaf children at one time were able to hear or to hear partly the tone-controlled voice of their teacher. Further tests showed that the hearing aid was a necessity for teaching children who were not more than sixty per cent deaf. As a result, three hearing-aid classes were formed in 1934. The results in these classes was so encouraging that in the following year the number of hearing-aid classes was increased to eight. By 1936 there were eleven such classes – including one in the Allen Homes.

By 1938 the hearing-aid programme was found to be so successful that work schemes were altered to bring the scope of subjects very close to that used in normal elementary schools. Then another experiment was carried out in which children were given individual microphones. With their use each child heard its own speech amplified and was heard by every other member of the class. The teacher was able to talk to individual children as she went round the class instead of going back each time to her own microphone. Every member of the class was aware of everything said by teacher or classmate from every point – as in a class of hearing children. Today this is normal procedure in deaf education, but at Margate at that time it was an important breakthrough which was taken up and developed by many other schools for deaf children.

The school had always taken an interest in the welfare of ex-pupils and in 1907 had established an After Care Fund for this purpose. The Fund was started with the sum of £361 realized by the sale of portraits of patrons, the Duke and Duchess of Gloucester painted by Sir William Beechey and presented to the school in 1845, but for a reason unrecorded, this money was never used for its intended purpose. Then in 1934, it was decided to put the fund into active operation and to raise extra money from the Chapel Fund. This fund was started in 1919 to build a chapel in the school grounds, but various obstacles over the years prevented this. Meanwhile the money was left to gather interest until it totalled £6,281.

In January 1934 a letter was sent to all subscribers asking sanction to use the Chapel Fund as After Care Fund. After stating the financial state of the Fund the letter continued:

> The Committee have been thoroughly into the religious training of the pupils at the School, and are convinced that it is adequately provided for. Services are regularly held by the Headmaster and his Assistant. The idea of building a Chapel has been definitely abandoned.
>
> It has been found that the most immediate need of our pupils is the establishment of an 'After Care Fund' from which grants could be made for the purchase of tools etc. to enable pupils to secure a reasonable start in life, and for Apprentice Fees.
>
> In order to avoid troubling you further I will assume your acquiescence unless I hear from you to the contrary.

Not all the subscribers to the Chapel Fund agreed but as a result, £2,700 of the chapel money was transferred to the After Care Fund.

Sporting facilities were much extended in 1934 with the building of a sports pavilion and a tennis court, and in 1936 a new gymnasium was opened by the Rt Hon Oliver Stanley, President of the Board of Education.

In 1937 a Parliamentary Bill was passed to lower the (compulsory) age of admission of children attending schools for the deaf from seven to five years. This led to the reorganization of the Margate Allen Homes to allow for the accommodation of twenty-five more children below the age of seven, and additional teaching and domestic staff. This brought the number of children in Allen Homes to seventy.

The School Farm was closed in 1938 after operating for twelve years, It had been started for the purpose of training boys and girls for a career in agriculture but the hopes that this form of training would be of value did not materialize. It was found that many parents were unwilling to allow their children to take up agriculture for a living. The result was that the cost of running the farm in relation to the numbers placed there became prohibitive. The farm land was converted into additional playing fields.

HIS MAJESTY KING GEORGE VI
HER MAJESTY QUEEN ELIZABETH
HER MAJESTY QUEEN MARY, THE QUEEN MOTHER

President:
The Archbishop of Canterbury

Vice-Presidents:
The Duke of Bedford
The Duke of Montrose
Earl Bathurst
Lord Charnwood
The Bishop of London
The Bishop of Norwich
The Bishop of Rochester
The Bishop of Wakefield
The Bishop of Winchester
The Bishop of Worcester
The Bishop of Dover
The Dean of Canterbury
The Dean of Salisbury
Major P.H.G. Powell-Cotton
Leonard Mortimer
A.W.Williams
The Duchess of Montrose
The Marchioness of Downshire
The Viscountess Portman
Lady Aldenham
Lady Hervey
Lady Mance

Royal Patronage and Presidency of
The Royal School for Deaf and Dumb Children in 1938:

From the 60s.

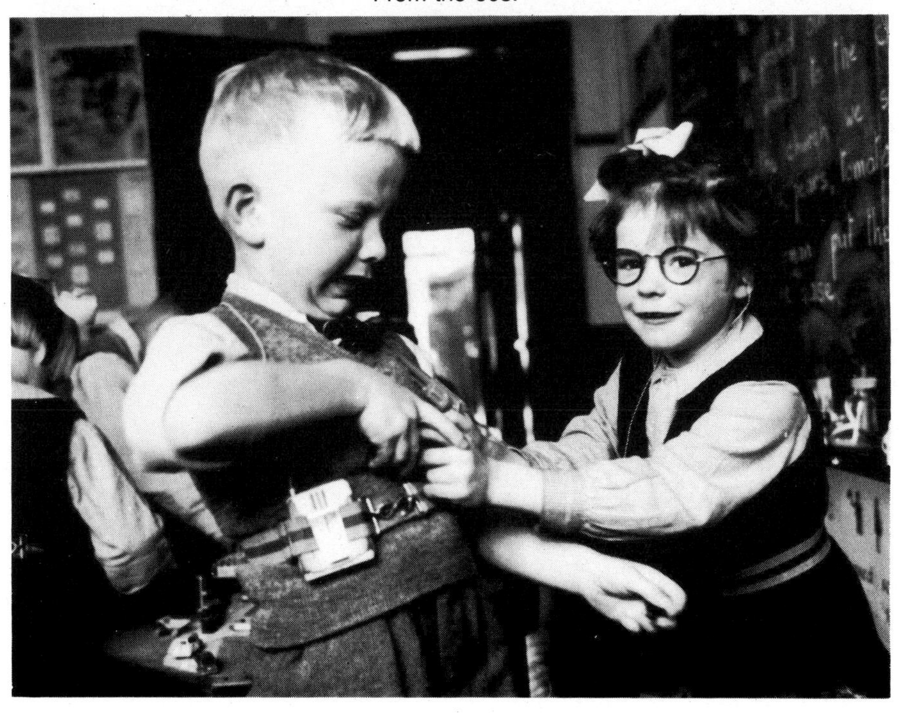

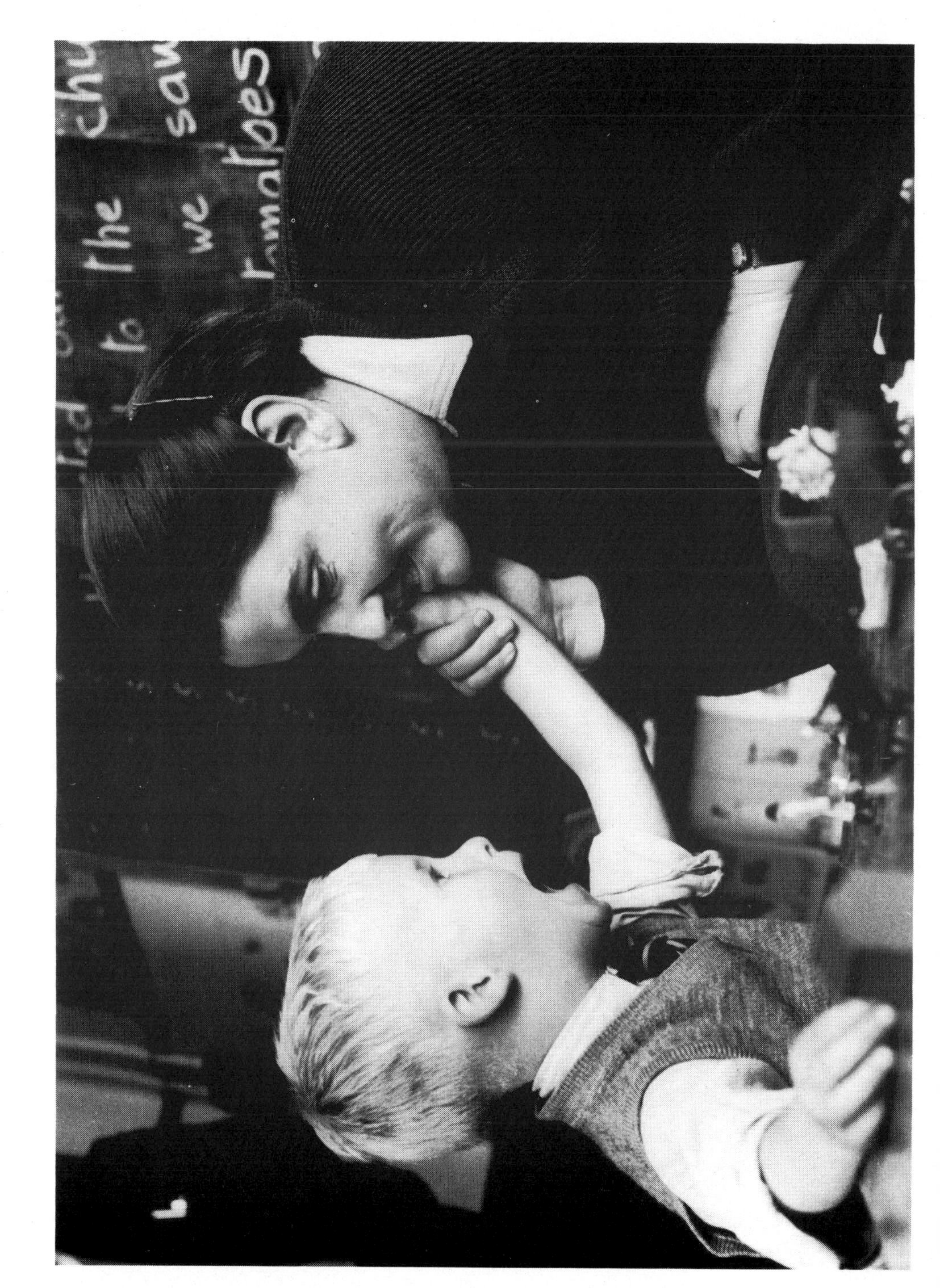

The old School being pulled down in 1972.

The new School.

Below: Sculpture of Christ healing a deaf man by Cyril Day ARCA.

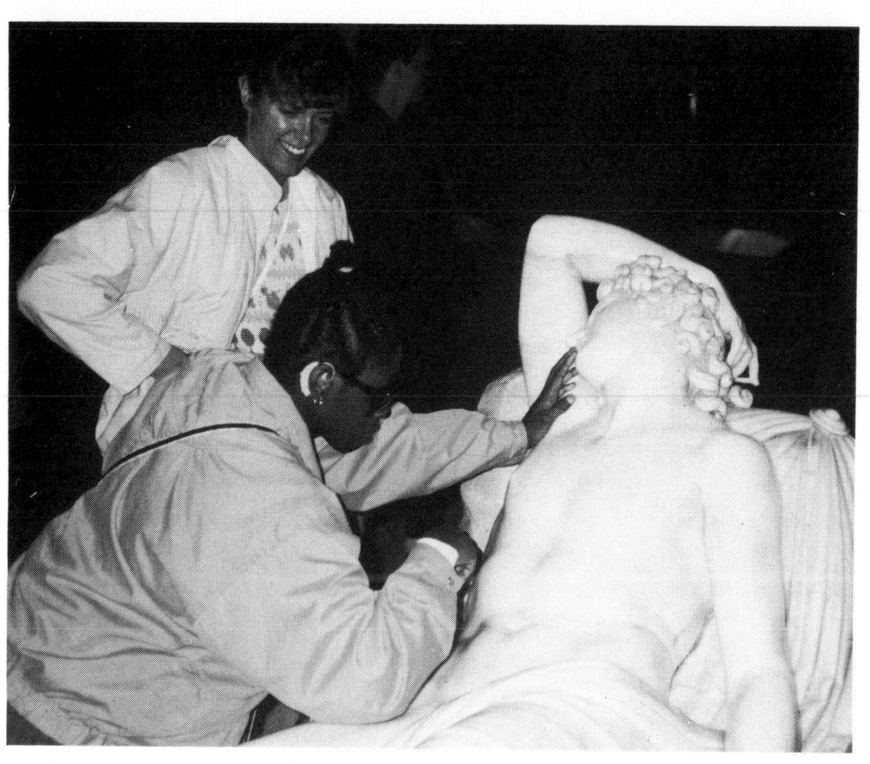

A deaf and blind girl investigates a sculpture at Chatsworth House.

Below: Computing.

A visit to Switzerland in 1987.

13

The Second War and After 1939–1968

What matters deafness of the ear, when the mind hears? The one true deafness, the incurable deaf ness, is that of the mind.
Victor Hugo

When the Second World War began in September 1939 there were 417 children at the school and all possible precautions were taken to secure their safety. Deep, spacious air-raid shelters were built, gas-masks were issued and the children trained in their use. The war was to have a far greater disruptive effect on the school than had the 1914–18 conflict. Some male teachers were mobilized, there was food-rationing and general shortages of everything. But during the nine months of the so-called 'phoney-war' which followed, the school routine continued normally. It was not until May 1940 when the Germans overran Holland and Belgium and opened the way for air attacks on southern England that the decision was made to evacuate the school.

The Oxfordshire village of Goring-on-Thames was chosen as the school's wartime location. Here three large houses were taken – Cariad, for the senior girls, The Grange, for intermediate children, and Nun's Acre, for the juniors. Accommodation for the senior boys was at Newnham Manor, near Wallingford, some five miles from Goring.

To facilitate the move it was decided to advance the start of the 1940 summer holiday from July to May and all children who were able to go to their homes in safety were sent there; this left some 130 pupils and the staff to be moved. The transporting of furniture, equipment, apparatus and stores of such a large school was a long, involved task which was carried out by road on May 28 and following days. When the task of re-assembling the school was completed it was found that the space required for dormitories, dining-rooms and staff rooms left insufficient accommodation for the classrooms. In consequence, the local vicarage, a villa and two garages were acquired. During September all the children who had been sent home were recalled as accommodation became available and at the start of the Autumn term the school re-opened in its unusual, scattered premises.

The school remained in Oxfordshire for a little more that five years and carried on successfully in spite of difficulties caused by restricted accommodation and the lack of many facilities enjoyed at Margate. During the evacuation period the children did their share of war work. Senior boys assisted the local farmers, and assembled to pack stores for a Royal Ordnance Depot in the Wallingford area. The senior girls helped the local Red Cross and worked on making camouflage nets for the army. The work of the staff was difficult in such makeshift premises and a great deal of improvising was necessary. But there were many compensations for staff and children alike, for all the houses had large grounds and beautiful gardens, and nearby was the Thames with its locks, weirs, boats and facilities for fishing and bathing.

The departure from Margate proved to be a wise move, for the school was hit by both high-explosive and incendiary bombs. The headmaster's house, the engineer's residence and the school lodge in Victoria Road were destroyed, and a bomb went through the apex of the school roof and caused extensive damage. But worst of all was the severe damage suffered by Allen Homes. This was a serious matter for it later resulted in a considerable reduction in the number of nursery children attending the school and consequently a long waiting list.

During the evacuation period, the Allen Home children were transferred to the main school with its comparatively stricter regimentation – an inclusion which was not desirable, as the younger children needed the special attention and facilities peculiar to their age. But the way in which they fitted in says much for the skill and care shown by the Allen Home staff.

In spite of the immense difficulties which resulted from the move, the education and welfare of the children did not suffer to any great extent – although, of necessity, some of the vocational training, such as printing and tailoring, were discontinued. But overall, the move to Goring was an achievement of which all the staff felt justly proud. It provided an opportunity for willing cooperation and unselfishness which strengthened the good-feeling which existed between all staff members.

Immediately following the Allied victory in Europe in August 1945, the school returned to Margate and re-opened for the Autumn term. During the war the buildings had been used by the Margate Corporation for a number of purposes which included Civil Defence headquarters and the accommodation of bombed-out people and there was much clearing up to be done when the school reopened. Many of the dormitories, staff rooms and classrooms were in a badly dilapidated state and the grounds had been neglected for some five years. For many months workmen were busy everywhere repairing ceilings, floors and windows.

At that time there was accommodation for up to 475 children, both profoundly deaf and partially hearing, but in 1946 the Board of Education decided that the number of pupils was excessive for the accommodation available and set the maximum number at 334. No pupils were to be admitted beyond that number, but pupils already in excess could remain. The reduction to 334 was achieved by not replacing 'leaving pupils' with new admissions. Two years later the important decision was made to segregate the profoundly deaf from the partially hearing. In the Autumn term of 1948 nine profoundly deaf children were transferred to Margate from Yorkshire Residential School for the Deaf at Doncaster, eight from Ovingdean Hall School for the Deaf at Brighton, two from the Exeter School for the Deaf and thirteen from the Newcastle School for the Deaf. Fourteen partially deaf children were moved from Margate to the Brighton school. The Margate intake was in addition to the normal number of starters for that year.

Also in 1946 came a change in the arrangements of the supply of hearing-aids. The school had long been equipped with hearing apparatus for various purposes and, until then, had relied on equipment produced by commercial manufacturers. No national system existed for ensuring that the apparatus came up to the highest standards or fitted the exact needs of the individual. Neither had there been any scheme for servicing hearing aids and this resulted in many problems. Government took a hand in this by appointing a committtee of a number of surgeons and specialists of Radar to report on the manufacture of hearing-aids. As a result, the government sponsored the manufacture and maintenance of hearing-aids of an approved standard. These aids were from thenceforth provided and maintained by government to schools for the deaf.

But there were still children whose hearing infirmities were beyond the help of electronics. Concerning the congenital deaf, it appears that outside Margate the old oral v signing controversy was still in progress some seventy years after the Milan Congress. But a passage in the school's Annual Report for 1950 shows that the Royal School still favoured the combined method of instruction. The words could well have been written by Richard Elliott himself.

> How the congenital deaf child may best be educated has been debated at length in the Deaf Press. Some teachers doubt whether education by the pure oral method which frowns on finger spelling and prohibits signs is the one and only way to educate the congenital deaf child who goes to an ordinary Deaf school. These

> teachers doubt that education by this method does or can enable him to lead the more or less normal life of a hearing person as is suggested by advocates of pure oralism in the Sunday Press. Most of those whose work is among the adult congenital deaf and the adult deaf themselves are sure that the pure oral method is neither the only way or the best way for the majority of congenital deaf children and that by following the pure oral method too rigidly the teachers miss the wood for the trees.

No extravagant claims for the profoundly deaf children were made by the Royal School. There it was seen, as it had always been, that there were pupils who could benefit from pure oral teaching and others who could not. The latter, who were in a large majority, were taught by a combination of oral and manual teaching and, as always, the congenital deaf children communicated with one another usually by signs, sometimes by finger-spelling and rarely, if ever, by voice and lip-reading.

The school's overall policy at that time was to concentrate on the teaching of language with speech and lip-reading as subsidiary subjects. Signs were used only when other means of communication – writing, printing, speech, lip-reading, finger-spelling and illustrations by chalk, pen or pencil failed. If used in any other way, signs were seen as a hindrance to the acquisition of language. In fact the teaching policy at Margate was leading the way to what is now known as Total Communication.

But whatever the method used, the aim of each teacher at the Royal School was to help the deaf child to become a well-integrated deaf individual rather than a pale imitation of a hearing person. If a child could not learn to read lips or speak intelligibly, the teachers allowed and encouraged him to develop other modes of expression and communication rather than send him into the world ashamed and frustrated because he could not acquire the difficult art of speech and lip reading. This policy is the same today.

Since 1945 the school had been taking a number of deaf children suffering from additional physical and mental handicaps. In 1954 the Ministry of Education suggested that the school should make provision to take more children under the age of five as well as more educationally sub-normal (ESN) children. There were some thirty children in the area still awaiting placement in addition to another eighty-three children on the waiting list for Penn and Bridgehouse school. The Headmaster agreed to accept more but the Committee did express concern to the Ministry that the Margate school should not have an over concentration of ESN children.

Early in 1956 the new Headmaster, Tom Pursglove, agreed to open a special department and called it an Opportunity stream.

1957 saw the death of Bill Swayne, who had been headmaster for twenty-three years. In addition to the valuable work he devoted to the Royal School – particularly during the difficult time of the evacuation – he contributed much to deaf education. In 1955 he published a Scheme for Teaching Language which included a new graded vocabulary which he devised. In 1956 he was awarded an OBE for his work with deaf children. Swayne was succeeded by Tom Pursglove, a Derbyshire man who began his career in deaf education in 1935 at the Yorkshire school for the Deaf in Doncaster. During World War Two he served with the RAF, was captured by the Japanese in Burma, escaped and was recaptured. On his return to Britain he became deputy-head of the Birmingham School for the Deaf, and from 1951 to 1956 was headmaster of the Nottingham School for the Deaf.

In 1958 an Act of Parliament was passed 'to confer further powers' on the school (ie. to increase its powers of investment) and to change its name to the Royal School for Deaf Children Margate – the words 'and Dumb' being finally removed.

On the 1st April, 1963 the school was registered with the Ministry of Education under Section 4 of the 1960 Charities Act. In 1974 the registration was transferred to the Charity Commissioners.

14

Rebuilding the School: 1968–1986

This school was founded in 1792. It is 180 years old. Last October the workmen started demolishing the school to build a new one. Why? Because it was a very old building.

Pupil at Royal School, 1972

The year 1986 saw the publication of the Lewis Report, the result of a four-year study carried out by a committee appointed by the Secretary of State for Education and Science on 'The Possible Place of Finger Spelling and Signing in the Education of Deaf Children'.

Never before had there been so thorough an investigation into the methods used in the education of deaf children and yet its conclusions and recommendations coincided with those that had long been held and practised at the Royal School. The Lewis Report was in fact to serve as an overall guideline in the conception and design of the new Royal School, since its publication came at a time when the Committee of Management was engaged in talks with the Department of Education on plans to demolish the old school and replace it with a modern complex for the accommodation of 120 profoundly deaf and 72 multiply handicapped and profoundly deaf children. By the late 1960s, many deaf children who once would have attended special schools for the deaf were being accommodated in mainstream schools, with the result that Margate had become far too large for the falling numbers of children being admitted. Then again, the century old Victorian-Gothic building was expensive to run and difficult to maintain; most of the classrooms were too small and not acoustically suitable for their purpose. Up-to-date, specially designed rooms had become necessary to help profoundly deaf children and, in particular, improved, modern amenities were urgently needed for the multiply handicapped pupils who since 1945 had made up an increasing proportion of the school's population.

The negotiations between the School and the Department of Education took place during 1968–69. They were prolonged but eventually successful with the Department agreeing to pay eighty per cent of the total cost of the development. The cost agreed with the Department was £10.60 a square foot, and it was fortunate that the school decided to rebuild at that time, for its cost today would be at least £75 a square foot, which would have amounted to some £5.6million instead of its actual cost of £800,000 – a sum that included all the furnishing and equipment. It was also most fortunate that the decision to rebuild came at a time when government was in a generous mood for the rebuilding of schools; had the decision been much delayed it could never have been implemented. In the event, the Department of Education contributed £600,000 of the money; the balance of £200,000 being raised by a public appeal.

Because the majority of the children came from London, the possibility of building the new school nearer to London was discussed and local authorities were consulted. But a geographical move presented many problems, not least the difficulties in securing a site within a town. The idea was eventually rejected – mainly because of the good relations that had been developed with Margate over the years, for the Royal School had long been part of the town's social life. Furthermore, its activities had become integrated with Margate's commercial community, with many local firms making work experience courses available to the older pupils.

Leslie Dale, a Margate chartered architect, was appointed for the design and completion of the new buildings and prior to starting work, he and the headmaster carried out a long programme of research. This included visits to other schools in the UK and Euskirchen, Dortmund, Bielefeld and Cologne in Germany to study the latest developments in deaf education. Detailed plans were then made for a total area of accommodation of some 70,000 square feet. One important feature of the overall design is the association of the buildings on a scale suitable for children which creates for them a feeling of belonging and unity. Some of the buildings were designed with asymmetrical roofs to the classrooms to create the necessary acoustic requirements and noise reverberation control, and all the teaching areas were installed with hearing-aid equipment. The early objection to the Margate site as being unhealthy for children had some basis, for it is on a very high ground and faces north. To counter this, the new design includes three totally enclosed courtyards, one of which is covered so that the children can go into the open air in winter.

W.W. Martin (Thanet) Limited, an old established Ramsgate building firm, secured the contract through competition and building operations began in 1972. The building programme was complicated and involved due to the problem of keeping the old school running normally whilst alterations were taking place – this resulted in considerable pressures on the staff, both teaching and domestic. Everywhere were cranes, excavators, dumpers and all the other paraphernalia of a major building operation with dust, dirt and noise penetrating the entire school. Another problem was the continuance of all services, such as heating, lighting, water, throughout the operations.

Credit is due to the school staff throughout the years of the reconstruction, for there was no disruption of teaching or any other of the school's functions. There were, of course, some alarming incidents. On one occasion a group of boys stood one of their number in a cement-mixer for the purpose of making him a pair of concrete boots. A teacher discovered them in the act of turning on the machine. But throughout the four-year operation there were no injuries to children or staff.

In 1975, the decision was made to close the London office, a move that was made with some regret, for it was the school's final break with the City of London where it was founded and had flourished for so many years.

At Margate the original plan had been to retain the existing entrance hall and the old fairy-tale tower which had been such a conspicuous feature of Margate town for over a century. With great generosity the building contractor offered to renovate the tower at cost price, but it was finally decided that this was a luxury the school could not afford and so it was demolished. But a memento of the old dining hall was preserved in the form of two of the angels which had gazed down on generations of Margate pupils. One presides in the White Wing and the other in the dining-room court. Four Victorian stained glass windows presented to the school in 1880 by the then Treasurer, Charles Few, are also preserved in the present dining-room. Over the main entrance to the school was placed a sculpture of Christ healing a deaf man. This is by Cyril Day ARCA of Canterbury, cast by Ray Evison of Canterbury College of Art and presented to the school by the architects. Beneath the sculpture is a plaque which records the miracle:

> According to St.Mark's Gospel, 'They bring unto him one that was deaf and had an impediment in his speech and they beseech HIM to put HIS hand upon him, and HE took him aside from the multitude and put his fingers upon his ears and HE spit and touched his tongue and looking up to heaven HE sighed and saith unto him 'EPHPHATHA' that is 'BE OPENED' and straightway his ears were opened and the strings of his tongue were loosed and he spake plain'.

During the course of the excavations for the new buildings, the foundations of the old St. John's College were revealed together with a lime-burner's kiln. Later there came to light all sorts of interesting objects which had been discarded as rubbish and used in the foundations. The children quickly became archaeologists and made a fine collection of Victorian jars, bottles and other items.

Also unearthed was evidence of a robbery which must have been committed in 1880. When the foundation stone commemorating the start of additional buildings was laid in July 1880, a number of contemporary items were put into a vacuum-sealed flask and placed beneath the stone. They included current coins of the realm (some of which were of gold), a list of the school governors and various newspapers of the day – including a copy of *Keble's Gazette* (later today's *Isle of Thanet Gazette*). Then, within a few days of the stone-laying and before the bricking-up was completed, someone dug down to the cavity, smashed the sealed jar and took the money; the papers were left. Luckily, a similar jar was found beneath another commemorative stone laid at the time. A teacher at the school commented: 'The theft was not necessarily committed by a workman. The whole of Margate knew about the ceremony and what was placed there.'

On October 3 1972 the commemorative stone of the new school was unveiled by the Treasurer, Lord Harris, and building started on the new department for the multiply handicapped, which was completed and occupied in 1973. This separate provision was essential to the aims of the school, and it has since been imitated elsewhere.

Early in 1976 the main buildings were completed and on April 2 the Queen Mother unveiled a commemorative plaque before an audience of distinguished visitors. Her arrival and departure on the school lawn in a red helicopter of the Queen's Flight was an especial thrill for the children.

The various buildings and other features of the new school were each named after a headmaster or other person who had given the school outstanding service:

School for Multiply Handicapped	Elliott Wing
Nursery and Infants School	Pursglove Wing
Homes	Allen Homes
Main Hall	Maltby Hall

Main Classroom and Residential Complex	White Wing
Main Courtyard and Cloisters	Harris Square
Hall and Dining Room Courtyard	Barkley Square
Courtyard at End of Dining Room	Swayne Square
Library	Stevens Library

The completion of the new school was the climax to the long career of Tom Pursglove. It is much to his credit that at a time when he was in sight of his retirement, he stayed on to play an important role with the architect in the designing and building of the new school. No such school had been built in Britain for many years and he had no rules or experience to guide him. Nevertheless, he immersed himself in the hard and demanding work involved with the full knowledge that there would be little or no part for him in the project when it was completed. Tom Pursglove was a man who devoted all his energies to the welfare of the school and he gave confidence to parents because he believed absolutely in what he was doing. He had a special concern for newcomers and would spend much of his time comforting them until they got over their home-sickness. Little children saw him as a playmate, the older as a figure of authority, but in the nicest sense. A keen and skilful cricketer, he did much to promote the game among the pupils. He kept the school in the forefront of the education of deaf children, and exercised a leading role in the profession as Chairman of the National College of Teachers of the Deaf in 1970. He contributed to teacher training under the auspices of the National College, by acting as external examiner for its examination board.

This involvement in professional affairs at national level, and the concern for new entrants, were exhibited equally by Brian Armstrong, who succeeded Tom Pursglove as Headmaster on his retirement in April 1976. In October of that year, the National College of Teachers of the Deaf was amalgamated with the Society of Teachers of the Deaf to form the British Association of Teachers of the Deaf: this new body was intended to represent the interests of all teachers of hearing-impaired children, whether they worked in special schools, the traditional province of the National College, or in the 'external services' from which the Society had recruited its members. Brian Armstrong and his staff played a significant part in ensuring that the British Association retained an in-service training Diploma for teachers of hearing-impaired children, in the early 1980s; and from 1984 to 1986 he was Association President.

On taking up his post, Brian Armstrong had been faced with what he and other staff members considered an important operation. One thing the school had never been able to shake off was the long established insulation from the rest of society suffered by residential schools for the deaf. It was urgently necessary to break out from this mould, to involve the school in the outside world and to create links with social workers and those other professionals who are ultimately responsible for sending children to Margate. The decision was made that Brian Armstrong would extend his commitment to the wider area of deaf education, whilst the school's secretary and bursar, Derrick Downs, involved himself and the school in the local scene.

For the children there was always a real danger of isolation: Richard Elliott had lamented that 'The Asylum was the children's life; they never left it except to go to church, from the day they entered to the day they left for the last time!' But when a Miss Mackintosh left the school £29,000 in 1975, the Committee of Management used it to establish a Mackintosh Travel Fund to enable parties of children to make tours both in the UK and abroad. The fund was increased by a further £24,000 in 1986, as a result of a legacy from a Miss Florence Adams. It then became known as the Mackintosh Adams Travel Fund, and it has allowed a broadening of experience and a widening of horizons for many Royal School pupils over the years. Travel abroad began in May 1976 when a party of twenty children and four staff made a nine-day tour of Switzerland. Since then summer holiday tours have become a regular feature of the school. In 1985 a party of children made an exchange visit to the National

Institute for Deaf Children in Paris. Other tours have included Austria in 1985, Switzerland (1987) and Canada (1978).

Travel closer to home brought tragedy within weeks of Tom Pursglove's impending departure from the school. In February 1976 there was an accident to a hired coach bringing forty-nine of the children and two escorts back to the school following a weekend at home. Stephen Holmes, a pupil aged twelve who had been at the school since the age of three, and the Matron, Mrs. Ethel Taylor, were killed. Sixteen pupils and a teacher were injured but all recovered. The rescue services of the police and ambulance could not understand at first why all the children were seemingly so calm. There was no screaming or shouting and it was thought that they were in a severe state of shock; they did not realize that the children were deaf. Tributes were paid to their courage, and to the willing support offered by many teachers, by rescue workers and hospital staff.

The years immediately following Brian Armstrong's appointment to the Royal School saw far reaching national developments in the field of special education. In 1978 the Warnock Committee of Enquiry into the Education of Handicapped Children and Young People published its Report, 'Special Educational Needs'. Foremost among its recommendations was the abolition of categories of handicap, and the principle that children with special educational needs should be integrated into the mainstream schools as far as was commensurate with efficient education of mainstream and 'special' pupils alike. Legal force was given to these and other recommendations by the Education Act of 1981. A decade later, the provisions of this Act continue to determine administrative practice in special schools, through the statementing, review and reassessment procedures.

In 1978, the year of publication of the Warnock Report, the school's first educational psychologist was appointed, to be involved in counselling and guidance, organization, educational and behavioural programming and curriculum development. For many years the emphasis on the assessment and training of young deaf children had increasingly relied on the audiological approach and on technical advances in many other sciences, including psychology, which led to a more realistic understanding of the problems of innate intelligence and language acquisition. Other disciplines brought in over the following years were physiotherapy and speech and language therapy.

Until 1983 there was no suitable place in the school for assessing the educational and therapeutic needs of handicapped children, but in that year a legacy was received from a Mrs. Hilda Gordon, whose sister was a pupil at the school from 1897–1906, and it was decided to use the money to establish an Assessment Centre. The sick bay had for some years proved to be too large for the current number of pupils and now one half was sound-proofed, acoustically altered and equipped for a new use. Named the Gordon Assessment Centre, it comprises an audiological assessment room, multi-purpose studio, technician's rooms, educational psychologist's office and assessment room, and the second Deputy Head's office which houses the staff training library. Another important development in audiological provision was the replacement in 1985 of all hard-wired group hearing aids with an infra-red amplification system which gives greater flexibility in use. The old group aids were not wasted but thoroughly overhauled and donated to overseas schools which were in urgent need of such equipment. Some went as far as Sri Lanka and Ethiopia.

Further refurbishments at the Royal School were made possible in 1986 by two donations; one from Mr. and Mrs. Pocock, in memory of their son, Stewart David, who had died in a motoring accident two years before at the age of twenty-two; and the other in memory of Tom Pursglove, who died in 1984. The money was used for work on the sports pavilion, which is a notable landmark at the corner of the school playing field and in constant use by the older pupils in particular. The first of the two gifts made possible the extension and modernization of the pavilion changing rooms, and the second paid for the overhaul of the attractive clock.

One area specifically addressed in the Warnock Report was that of Further Education. During the 1970s, many pupils had remained at the Royal School until reaching the age of eighteen or nineteen, and it was felt that they would benefit from living and working in a different environment before leaving – one that would encourage them to develop independence in the conduct of their lives. So the decision was made in 1978 to establish off-site accommodation to house those senior pupils attending further education and work-experience programmes outside the school. It was to be so organized that it would be seen by pupils as something separate from the institutional feeling that is inseparable from a large residential school – a half-way house, as it were, towards life in the outside world. Following a lengthy search, a small hotel was purchased for £50,000 in Westgate, a quiet residential town three miles from the school.

Although geographically distant, Westgate Lodge is administered by the Royal School and its management is the responsibility of the school's Post-16 Co-ordinator. In 1979 it was the first unit of the school's Further Education Department to offer courses to students. In 1984 came the purchase, alteration and final occupation of a new department known as Brook House. This provides for multiply-handicapped children similar facilities to those of Westgate Lodge. Situated in Westbrook, the unit provides Further Education for students up to the age of nineteen. The original plan was that the students would spend most of the time within the house learning life-skills, but this was soon extended to include attendance at a wide variety of specially designed courses at Canterbury Technical College.

This move was followed by the institution of the Brook House Programme with its sheltered workshop facilities in a part of the St. John's Trust premises at Margate. All Brook House students are given the opportunity to use the workshops, but priority is given to those who are unlikely to be able to find employment on the open market. During workshop sessions, students work at their own pace at a variety of crafts under the supervision of qualified instructors. Starting from raw materials, finished articles are produced by the student for pleasure, for their own use or for sale, thereby encouraging confidence, concentration and pride in the finished product. The St. John's Trust building is also used to encourage local people to set up small businesses, so the Brook House workshops are in an effective working environment.

There was further development at Westgate Lodge in 1986 when the large adjoining house was purchased and converted into self-contained bedsitter flats for senior students as a further step towards independent living. There is also residential accommodation for staff. Students in their second year of Further Education live here and cater and budget for themselves. An important feature of this development is the requirement that students who have in many cases spent their entire school lives in a residential environment are put in the position of looking after themselves, and coming to terms with domestic responsibilities. The house was named Venn House, as the purchase was greatly helped by a generous legacy from Mrs Beatrice Venn. It has since become an intrinsic part of the old school's post-16 provision.

Students residing at Venn House, Westgate Lodge and Brook House are encouraged to mix with the community, join clubs, attend evening classes and develop their own interests. Each year an expedition/adventure course is arranged and other similar activities are planned throughout the year. Contact and friendships at home are maintained by regular weekend visits.

Since the opening of the new school in 1976, management and staff have not rested content and there has been an on-going programme of improvements and up-grading which still continues. The Allen Homes have been refurbished, the swimming-pool glass-fibred and equipped with a new heat-exchange system and residential accommodation for senior boys greatly improved. Extensive works have been carried out to ensure that all children under the age of eleven and all multiply-handicapped children live in totally self-contained units where they are cared for by specialist staff. Areas of the school designed as staff accommodation have increasingly been taken over for use by children, as staff residential responsibilities have changed and as different groups of pupils with particular social needs have been identified.

In the early 1970s local authorities were pressing the Committee of Management to have representation on the governing body, but the Management Committee had resisted the move through fear that it could develop into a take-over by those authorities. However, some people could see benefits to the school if the Committee could be persuaded to accept at least a small representation of local authorities – even though the rules of the school precluded them from becoming full members of the Committee. In 1974 the Committee was eventually persuaded to invite representatives of the Kent Education Committee and the Inner London Education Authority as observers to Management Committee meetings; they had no voting rights, but were able to join in discussions and give advice. From this first, rather hesitant step there evolved a distinct trust between the school and those two authorities – to the extent that when these representatives retired from their jobs, they were elected as full members of the Committee of Management.

In 1985 the government introduced legislation compelling governing bodies of state schools to have teacher and parent representation – and government policies encouraged non-maintained schools to do the same. There is, however, an obstacle to this, for charity law prohibits paid employees of a charity from serving on its governing body. This prevented the election of Margate teachers to the Committee of Management. To solve this problem, the Committee of Management was redesignated as a board of Trustee Governors and a new governing board comprising 'school governors' was created. They were elected from teachers, educational assistants, child-care personnel and domestic workers. These School Governors meet twice a year with the power to make requests and representations to the Trustee Governors who meet monthly.

In 1977 a number of Local Education Authorities in the South of England requested that the Royal School should establish a regional facility for deaf blind children. The school responded to this and in 1979 established its unit for severely multi-handicapped deaf children, and hearing-impaired children with visual handicaps. The unit consists of a self-contained block of classrooms and other teaching rooms, and caters for children aged between four and twelve. A senior department takes these pupils on to school-leaving age. The unit was originally opened with thirteen children and this number was maintained until the staff had developed the necessary expertise. Within a little more than ten years it has become a major growth area.

Developments at the Royal School have reflected international, as well as regional and national concerns. In the late 1970s there was a gradual change of attitude regarding methods of communication in the education of deaf children. The efficacy of oralism was yet again being challenged. The US was in the forefront of this movement and various systems of signing were evolving. The Royal School had for some time maintained an open attitude to this matter and was sympathetic to the current trends. In 1979, the school adopted the philosophy of Total Communication as defined by Dr. David M. Denton, Superintendent of the Maryland School for the Deaf, when he visited Britain in 1976. This philosophy allowed a flexible approach to suit each individual child. As appropriate, emphasis may be on the spoken word, Signed English, Signs Supporting English, British Sign Language and/or gesture. This allows the teacher and the child maximum opportunity to communicate and to develop reading and writing skills. The policy ensured that the Royal School could offer to deaf children and their parents a particular type of educational provision not available elsewhere in the region. Throughout the 1980s and beyond, referrals to the school have confirmed the need for such a facility; and experience within the school has indicated the extent to which individual children can benefit from it.

From its beginnings the Royal School has always looked to

the future lives of its children. Many schools rightly advertize the achievements of their more brilliant pupils. But at Margate there is a conviction that real achievement is revealed when a school takes note of those who will never be able to reach academic success, and teachers concentrate much effort to help those who are in greatest need.

How would John Townsend, Henry Cox Mason and Henry Thornton react if they could see what has grown from the asylum 'for the support and education of the deaf and dumb children of the poor' they founded so long ago? Perhaps they would be most pleased and impressed by the way in which the Royal School is carrying out their object of benefiting those children who would have 'lived in misery and died in ignorance had there not been a charity of this kind existing'.

And what would Richard Elliott think if he could make a tour of the school that stands on the site of the ramshackle old Margate Workhouse?

The Royal School has had an eventful and sometimes chequered history, but throughout its two hundred years its energetic, progressive spirit had prevailed and there can be no doubt that the school will continue to lead in its field for as long as deaf children need its help.

THE SCHOOL TODAY

by

Julie Gemmill
A member of the teaching staff

Today the Royal School for Deaf Children Margate is a non-maintained residential special school, governed by four Acts of Parliament and registered as a charity. It has no particular religious or other affiliations, and accepts pupils from all parts of the world, but it serves mainly as a regional resource for the south and south-east of England, and the Channel Isles. It offers seven-day boarding facilities, and the majority of the pupils spend every second weekend at home. Children living within a reasonable distance can travel home every weekend, and there is always a small proportion of day pupils with homes in Thanet and the surrounding area. The total number of pupils and students on roll in January 1992, between the ages of five and nineteen, is 167.

At each stage of a child's education the school provides him or her with a Total Communication environment which extends well beyond the classroom. All teaching and care staff are expected to undertake appropriate training in communication skills, and a continuous programme is organized to meet their varying needs, by the Communication Coordinator. Classes are provided at different levels, including induction courses for those who join the school staff with no previous experience of sign language. Candidates are prepared for assessment in Signs Supporting English and in Signed English, in accordance with nationally recognized criteria. The school has been involved in the Working Party for Signed English from its inception, with senior members of staff contributing to regular discussion of practicalities as well as to policy decisions. Signed English was at one time promoted within the Royal School as the method of communication for use with all classes, but this policy was modified in the light of experience, and Signed English is now used in formal language teaching situations only, particularly to assist in the development of reading and writing. The form of signing universally used for communication purposes is Signs Supporting English, which draws extensively on British Sign Language.

A particularly important contribution to signing skills in the school as a whole is made by members of staff who are themselves deaf (in some cases former pupils) and who provide role models for the children as well as practical guidance for their hearing colleagues. Outreach into the local community is achieved by members of the school staff teaching sign language courses at an adult education centre in Margate; and the use of Signed English is both taught and assessed, on a fairly regular basis, at schools and centres further afield. Termly Communication Days provide classes at the requisite levels for parents, many of whom travel long distances to maintain this essential link with their children's education. Families living locally have the opportunity of attending weekly evening classes in school, and these also meet the training needs of anyone engaged in voluntary work with the children.

Volunteers make a significant contribution to the work of the school, and at any one time there are likely to be people from different walks of life involved in classroom and residential duties on a voluntary basis. They will include participants in schemes such as Service Away from Home and the Duke of Edinburgh's Award, but where the placement does not form part of a programme of this kind, it often proves to be the first step towards paid employment in the school.

Responsibility for the children outside school hours is now solely in the hands of the child care staff. Previously, teachers were required by their contracts to fulfil a number of hours of 'duty' in the evenings or at weekends. In 1989 this requirement was removed, but teachers are still encouraged to take charge of groups of youngsters in leisure time for the purpose of following a particular interest. Care staff organize a large variety of activities, both on and off the school site. Especially at weekends, the minibuses which belong to the school are well used for visits all around the area; they are a familiar sight at local places of interest and in the carparks of popular sporting facilities.

Simultaneously with their assumption of total responsibility for the management of leisure time, child care staff were offered a new career structure in the school. The position of Head of Care was created, to supervize all child care work throughout the school. At the next level of seniority, two Deputy Heads of Care were appointed: one to be concerned with the care of children in the main school residences, and the other with the care of multi-handicapped pupils in their seven smaller home units. Another important way in which the status of child care staff is enhanced is with the provision of an in-service training course which is accredited within the school. This was initiated in the early 1980s, and is organized by the Head of Care, who secures contributions as appropriate from different members of staff, as well as organizing visits to other establishments. The course is not obligatory for care staff, but obtaining the Royal School's certificate affects the candidate's salary grade.

In the case of teaching staff, there is a legal requirement that a course of training in the teaching of hearing-impaired children must be successfully completed within three years of appointment, if the teacher is not already specially qualified in this field. The school-based in-service training which Brian Armstrong and his staff fought successfully to retain as an essential option for the profession has now been replaced by a distance learning Diploma cöurse operated by the University of Birmingham. In spite of the radical change in style, the new course continues to depend for its theoretical and practical components on the support of the Head and staff of the school, and this is always readily forthcoming. Brian Armstrong's personal commitment to the course had extended to acting as External Examiner, since April 1991.

Diploma candidates are required to undertake a placement of several weeks in another school which can provide contrasting experience of teaching hearing-impaired children. Similarly, the one-year full-time courses of training which are offered at several centres in the U.K. involve periods of teaching practice in different types of establishment, and the Royal School regularly provides placements for candidates requiring experience in a special school. The departments for multi-handicapped pupil are a potential source of experience of a more specialized kind of teaching, and periods of practice have been made available, in 1989–90 and 1990–91, to candidates on a course of training relating to the needs of multi-sensory impaired pupils. In addition the school has provided training opportunities for individual visitors from overseas, in the areas of hearing aid technology and audiological assessment, as well as in teaching.

In the course of any one year the number of visitors to the school is considerable: with backgrounds in either teaching or child care, they come as individuals or in groups, to further a particular interest or to observe the work of the school as a whole. By no means all of these visitors are students in training: in 1991, for example, the school played host to groups of prominent professionals from Finland and the USSR. Of equal importance was the visit, in the same year, of a group of deaf children from the national school of Paris: this was designed to follow up a previous visit there by a group of Royal School senior pupils, and it is hoped that this link will be maintained and strengthened in the future.

Apart from providing basic training as required for its staff, the Royal School supports attendance at a wide variety of in-service courses, mainly in the local area. By this means it has been possible for teaching staff to benefit from the experience of those working in mainstream schools, with regard particulalry to the implementation of the National Curriculum. Since 1989, this has increasingly become a major issue for discussion and a focus for development, as Statutory Orders for the foundation subjects have been published and national assessment arrangements have been put into effect. As a non-maintained special school, the Royal School is not legally required to implement the National Curriculum: however, it was recognized that it could only hope to retain the confidence of the Local Education Authorities which refer pupils to it by taking account of the demands of the Education Reform Act 1988, in so far as they could be seen to apply to its situation. Accordingly the school has committed itself to a programme of ongoing curriculum development in line with the statutory requirements for the core and other foundation subjects, and teaching staff have devoted a great deal of time and energy to this undertaking.

The process necessitated the restructuring of the teaching departments in main school in September 1990, to take account of the universally recognized organization of the years of compulsory schooling into four Key Stages. The Royal School's Primary School now caters for children aged five to eleven, and this covers Key Stages 1 and 2. Key Stage 3 begins with the move into the secondary department, which is divided into Lower School for the first two years and Upper School for ages thirteen to sixteen. Key Stage 4 ends at the age of sixteen, and assessment at that stage, in all schools, will largely take the form of GCSE examinations. These are offered, in several subjects, to suitable candidates at the Royal School, but other examinations are also made available, if they are thought to be appropriate: a particular example is the Royal Society of Arts examination in the Communicative Use of English for the Hearing Impaired.

The principle has been adopted throughout the Royal School that teaching and assessment under the National Curriculum will be implemented to the extent that they are seen adequately to serve the needs and reflect the capabilities of the pupils concerned. Actual disapplication of any part of the National Curriculum is avoided as far as possible, but it has been agreed that the school will not introduce the teaching of a modern language at Key Stages 3 and 4. (Nevertheless, knowledge of European culture, and an acquaintance with the French language in particular, will continue to be encouraged by visits abroad and the forging of links with other schools.) In the case of multi-handicapped pupils, assessment by Standard Assessment Tasks in the core subjects is likely to prove impracticable and, indeed, invalid. Level 1 in the National Curriculum is set too high to be relevant for many of the Royal School children, and for those capable of achieving at that level, the Statements of Attainment are too wide in scope to allow realistic assessment of continuous progress to be made. The school's response to this state of affairs, in conjunction with the staffs of other non-maintained schools for hearing-impaired children, has been to develop a set of Introductory Levels for English, Mathematics and Science, for use in the assessment of children's attainment: and to divide up the Statements of Attainment at Level 1 and beyond, to provide a series of small incremental steps against which progress can be recorded.

The drawing together of schools which are geographically far apart but which provide for very similar populations of children has been one of the most positive outcomes of the Royal School's response to the Education Reform Act. Continuing benefits can be expected from this situation in 1992, since plans for further shared work, on cross-curricular themes, are already in hand. Several of the other non-maintained schools are like the Royal School in having special departments for pupils with learning difficulties in addition to hearing impairment. Concern about these pupils in particular has resulted in valuable contacts being made with schools for children with severe learning difficulties, through attendance at national conferences and through dissemination of the Introductory Level documentation.

The Royal School's department for multi-handicapped youngsters between the ages of five and thirteen has expanded considerably in recent years. Enquiries, preliminary visits and referrals for placement occur throughout each term, originating from a wide geographical area: the provision clearly fulfils a need. An extension to the building in which these children are taught (in small class groups, with an average adult: child ratio of one to two) was opened in January 1990, to provide additional classrooms as well as a large Cookery Room and a specially designed area for Music and Movement. As well as the more traditional 'movement' activities, massage and aromatherapy have been introduced into the curriculum, and have proved beneficial, as well as very popular with the children. A further innovation is the use of hydrotherapy: a special pool has been incorporated into the building, with timetabled access. This is just one feature of the increased physiotherapy services which have been made available within the school as a whole, in response to the increasing severity and complexity of the medical conditions presented by pupils in all departments. The situation is regarded as a challenge, and it has significant implications for staffing, in both the short and the long term.

Throughout the school there is now a high proportion of pupils with visual problems, ranging from the need to wear glasses to correct vision, to total blindness. One teacher had advisory responsibility for all these youngsters, and works closely with a consultant opthalmologist who makes regular visits to the school. A child with a severe visual handicap but no additional learning difficulties will be placed in a main school class alongside normally sighted peers, and the appropriate adaptations will be made to lesson preparation and teaching materials. However, the majority of severely visually impaired children are placed in the departments for multi-handicapped pupils, and grouped there according to their needs.

For multi-handicapped youngsters, transfer to the senior stage of schooling takes place at the age of thirteen, and to the Further Education programme at Brook House, if appropriate, at the age of sixteen or over. When a student reaches nineteen, statutory responsibility for his of her welfare passes from the Local Authority to the Social Services Department in the home area. The difficulties which this stage presents, especially for parents, have long been recognized at the Royal School. Senior staff, particularly the Specialist Educational Psychologist, were instrumental in setting up a pilot scheme, in January 1990, to secure residential provision for deaf multi-handicapped young adults in Canterbury and Thanet. The scheme is funded by a grant from the local Social Services Department and the Health Authority, and line managed by the Royal National Institute for the Deaf. Office accommodation is provided in the school's Further Education Department at Westgate Lodge. At the start of its third year of operation, there are clear plans for the long-term development of this important initiative.

Expansion of the Royal School has not been limited to the specialist area of provision for multi-handicapped children and adults. The main school departments have maintained or even increased their numbers, at a time when other special schools for hearing-impaired children have been faced with possible or certain closure. The latter situation has in fact been responsible for a small number of recent referrals to the Royal School, at the secondary stage. In the majority of cases, however, it may be assumed that alternative forms of provision have proved inappropriate. Children have frequently been placed in units for hearing-impaired pupils attached to mainstream schools, where communication is solely by speech and lipreading, with the use of personal hearing aids and classroom amplification systems. A child who fails to develop a command of oral language on this basis is at a severe disadvantage, and is likely eventually to exhibit behavioural as well as learning problems.

The more flexible policy on communication adopted by the Royal School facilitates better understanding for these children, both of educational content and of personal feelings and relationships, and ensures a more rewarding experience of school life for them. It may be expected that the progressive implementation of the Education Reform Act will contribute positively to the future rate of referral, through the operation of Local Management of School and the publication of the results of National Curriculum assessment. In a plainly competitive atomosphere, the presence in mainstream schools of pupils with special educational needs may be considered unwelcome; and in staffing terms alone it will be increasingly difficult for these schools to deliver the broad and balanced curriculum to which hearing-impaired pupils are legally entitled.

One area of the curriculum in which the Royal School has particular strengths is Physical Education. The school is well equipped for a range of indoor and outdoor activities, and the facilities are well used, in P.E. lessons and in the children's free time. Swimming is a major leisure activity, but in addition, swimming lessons are timetabled weekly for all teaching departments. The practicality of teaching swimming to all pupils at Key Stage 1 has commanded considerable attention in the consultation process regarding Physical Education in the National Curriculum, and it is clear that the Royal School's on-site swimming pool is an invaluable asset. The overall programme of physical activities corresponds well to the Proposals for Physical Education for ages 5 to 16, published by the Department of Education and Science in August 1991, including the opportunity which is offered to older main school pupils each summer to take part in a week's course at an outdoor adventure centre. Children of all ages and abilities exhibit enthusiasm and prowess at the school's annual Swimming Sports (in March) and Sports Day (in July). Throughout the year, team fixtures are arranged with local groups of hearing youngsters, and the school is represented at sporting events organized for deaf children on both a regional and a national basis.

The widespread use of drama in the Royal School curriculum is similarly in line with current national requirements. Although not designated as a foundation subject in the National Curriculum, Drama is recognized as having a unique contribution to make; for deaf children it offers special opportunities of self-expression, communication and understanding. Lessons in different subject areas, for Royal School pupils of all ages, may involve mime and role play, and timetabled sessions with senior classes allow for the development of these skills. For special occasions, performances complete with costumes and props are prepared: these range from simple presentations of nursery rhymes or fairy tales to the full-scale pantomimes on traditional themes for which the school has become locally renowned. Involvement in a Christmas pantomime provides children with unparalleled experience of sustained teamwork. This in turn enhances their appreciation of the performances which are brought to the school, whenever an appropriate opportunity arises, by visiting educational theatre groups. The culmination of dramatic endeavour, for nine teenagers in main school, coincided remarkably with the bicentennial anniversary. At the end of 1990, the school was approached by a BBC producer seeking to cast a group of schoolboys in a play about the life of a deaf French nobleman, the Count of Solar. The Count was educated at the school for the deaf children in Paris at the time of the French Revolution, using manual methods of communication, and the boys concerned had to be fluent in the use of sign language. Thanks to the willing co-operation of teaching and care staff, they fulfilled a demanding schedule of rehearsals and filming at the BBC studios in London in February and March of 1991, with minimal disruption to their educational programme. The recorded play was broadcast on network television early in 1992.

The screening of *The Count of Solar* will no doubt have contributed to the raising of awareness of the needs of deaf people, in society as a whole. A great deal has already been achieved in this respect by the use of subtitles, and the presence of sign language interpreters, on television programmes. These developments have owed much in their turn to the public relations initiatives of such bodies as The Royal National Institute for the Deaf, The British Deaf Association, the Deaf Broadcasting Campaign and Breakthrough Trust Deaf-Hearing Integration. Deaf school-leavers now enter a different world from that which awaited previous generations, and they rightly bring very different aspirations to it. Technological advances ensure that information, and the participation in society which it enables, are becoming steadily more accessible to deaf adults.

The Royal School seeks to prepare its older pupils for these opportunities principally by making them computer literate to as high a level as possible: and also by giving them experience of making telephone calls using the Minicom. It also supports, each year, a Leavers' Course run by The Royal Association in Aid of Deaf People where many of the staff members are themselves deaf. Pupils in the final year of Upper School thus gain insights which should help them to find their way into adult society and eventually to take their place in it with confidence. Some ex-pupils of the Royal School will undoubtedly become leaders in the deaf community and will help to determine its future stance. It is of the greatest importance that the increasing self-awareness of deaf young people should not engender divisive attitudes, but should allow for recognition of achievement in all spheres and at all levels, in a society which includes people who are deaf, hearing and multi-handicapped.

Two major development projects are planned for the immediate future. Following the replacement of the central heating system and hot water system, a Technology Suite will be created in the former boiler house on the school site. This will enable teachers and pupils at the school to fulfil the requirements of Technology in the National Curriculum: the accommodation at present available for the contributory subjects does not allow an adequate degree of integration. The Attainment Targets in this new subject are designed to offer important learning opportunities to all pupils, and to demand the practice of a variety of thinking and practical skills. A wholehearted commitment to its implementation will result in benefits which will operate across the curriculum and throughout a wide age-range.

The school's abiding aim of ensuring that individual potential is fulfilled influenced the decision to pursue the second project, namely the acquisition of a farm. When a farm was previously owned by the Royal School, its main purpose was to provide vocational training opportunities for pupils who might find a lifetime's employment in agriculture. The opportunities currently envisaged relate more closely to the pupils' school lives. They include an extensive coverage of National Curriculum core subjects and cross-curricular themes, the benefits of first-hand experience of caring for animals and growing crops, and potentially vital contributions to the personal development of pupils of all capabilities.

As well as seeing the start of these long-term projects, the year 1992 has inevitably had its own special highlights. The first of these, in March, was the production by a group of school staff and friends of the play by William Gibson, *The Miracle Worker*, about Helen Keller and her teacher. One weekend in June comprised a service of thanksgiving in Canterbury Cathedral and an Open Day at the school for parents, friends and former pupils. The culmination of the Summer Term celebrations, in late July, was the visit of the school's royal patron, Her Majesty Queen Elizabeth the Queen Mother. Her Majesty's previous visit, in April 1976, commemorated the completion of the new school buildings; the period since then has noticeably been one of almost continuous development, in response to changing needs within the school and new pressures from outside.

A Chinese proverb says that paths are made by those who walk on them: the Royal School may confidently be expected to continue creating new paths for its pupils, as it enters its third century.

APPENDIX 1

(The Warnock Report)

From a speech by Brian Armstrong,
the present headmaster, (July 1978)

Brian Armstrong began by reviewing the concern that many in Special Education had felt concerning the 1976 Education Act, Section 10. This section gave to parents the right for their children to be educated in their own home schools, and, he said, for some this had seemed the 'death knell of children who could not cope in these situations'. Although the Act was fairly specific that some children would need special help, the danger was felt that some local authorities would interpret it as a way of saving money without actually considering the needs of the children. He continued:

Another thing that appeared was the Warnock Report, and the one thing this emphasized was that, while there was a need for integration, there was also a need for many of our children to be educated in the field of special education. It was interesting to note that it acknowledged that many parents were put under far too much pressure from the press and the other bodies, who implied that by sending their child to a special school they were, in effect, rejecting the child – a thing we know is not the case and that many parents sent them for one reason, the educational and social well-being of the child.

We had been worrying about the effects of the Act and the Report for some time but now we have to look at the future and it seems that we have a future, though there are certain things mentioned in the report which we have to do something about.

We are told that in Special Education and Special Schools we have been too insular and have not become a sufficient part of the community we live in. Nor have we made sufficient links with the schools around and with 'normal' hearing children.

However, we are delighted with one of our pupils who has started a course at a local secondary school in Ramsgate. All things start in little ways and that, to us, is a start for children who are able and capable to go out in the community, and take part in more normal things and follow courses which we are not able to provide here.

Another thing the report is rather scathing about is the standard of careers guidance and follow up, and links between home and school. Accordingly we have recently appointed a member of the staff to have specific responsibility for careers guidance. We are now beginning to build up links with careers workers in an effort to place our children correctly when they leave school. We are looking into the situation of work experience. We have a number of children who ought to stay on after the age of sixteen and some require a continuation of the normal course. For the majority, we have to rethink whether we are going to benefit them if we do that, or whether we need to prepare them for a working environment. We are delighted that two of our pupils have started going to work in a local factory to see what it is all about. These are things we have to develop in the near future.

We have been asked recently if we will consider setting up a unit for children who are deaf and blind. No one doubts the magnitude of this task and there is a pressing need for such a unit. We are investigating possibilities. This is a project which would start off in a very small way, but it is something that could grow. At one end of our school we would have children with massive additional handicaps, while at the other there would be children whom we would be getting out into the normal mainstream.

When we consider our future, we must think about communication. Today, when we look at methods of communication we find confusion, as there are so many systems. We appear to be entering a phase when there is not only a problem of the deaf communicating with the hearing, but also of the deaf communicating with the deaf. Here in this school we believe in total communication. By this we mean that we have oral communication in that we try to get the children to lipread as much as they can, and to use their hearing as much as they can. We believe in oralism, with the use of hearing supplemented by the British Deaf Sign language and finger spelling. Today we take in a great many children who are basically not communicating with anyone at all, and have no language or communication. Thus we start from zero and see where we go from there. In many cases the children concerned are seven, eleven or even thirteen years old.

Many parents ask us whether they should learn sign language and our answer is 'yes'. When they ask us how do they learn it our answer is 'we do not know' and that is the tragedy of the situation. We do think that the organization of classes must be at a local level. It is through the demands of the parents to teachers and social workers for the deaf that we will be able to know their needs and make the appropriate efforts to help.

Finally, a word about communication. What we need to do is to make the best possible use of the hearing we have. Recently there has been an improvement in the hearing aid situation. Gradually we will move through the school seeing that each child has a hearing aid more suited to his loss. We in school spend much time saying 'Please wear your hearing aid'. Parents too, have a part to play. The Warnock Report talks about parent partnership and we have got to work together. It is not easy to say 'No, this is something that will help you and you must wear it' to a child who comes home and wants to take off his aid, but unless we work together over this we are wasting our time. The children know our attitude in school. Let them see that the parents' attitude is the same at home.

In conclusion, the Warnock Report has one message for us, and that is that we in the schools must prove our worth. It is up to us to make sure that we prove to the world at large, and the educational system in particular, that what we can do is not just as good as anyone else, but that it is better. This is what we are hopefully and constantly striving to be – not a place just as good as, but a place that is better than anywhere else.

APPENDIX 2

List of Royal Visits

LONDON

1807 Foundation stone of Kent Road Asylum laid by The Duke of Gloucester

1811 The Duke of Gloucester visited the Asylum

1816 The Duke and Duchess of Gloucester visited the Asylum

1817 Queen Charlotte accompanied by Princess Elizabeth and the Duke and Duchess of Gloucester visited the Asylum and accepted the title of Protectress of the Asylum for the Deaf and Dumb Children of the Poor

1820 The Duchess of Kent, Princess Tudor and Prince Charles visited the Asylum

KENT

1875 The Prince of Wales opened the Margate Asylum accompanied by the Princess of Wales and Prince Waldemar of Denmark

1917 Princess Alice, Countess of Athlone, visited the school

1926 The Prince of Wales (later King Edward VII) visited the school

1930 Prince and Princess Arthur of Connaught vistied the school

1950 Lord Cornwallis, the Lord Lieutenant of Kent, and Lady Cornwallis visited the school

1951 The Princess Elizabeth, Duchess of Edinburgh, visited the school

1976 Her Majesty, Queen Elizabeth, The Queen Mother opened the new school buildings on completion of the redevelopment and rebuilding

APPENDIX 3

Patrons, Presidents and Officers

Patrons	1807/1834	The Duke of Gloucester
	1834/1857	The Duchess of Gloucester
	1858/1862	The Prince Albert the Prince Consort
	1867/1910	The Prince of Wales, later King Edward VII
		King George V
	1910/1936	Queen Mary
	1910/1953	King Edward VIII
	1936	King George VI: Queen Elizabeth
	1939/1952	Queen Elizabeth the Queen Mother
	1952	
Presidents	1815	Duke of Buckingham
	1827	Archbishop of Canterbury
	1844/1884	Duke of Buccleuch
	1884 to date	Successive Archbishops of Canterbury
Treasurers	1792/1814	Henry Thornton Esq MP
	1814/1853	Wm.Nottidge Esq
	1853/1877	Beriah Drew Esq
	1877/1886	Charles Few Esq
	1887	T L Bristowe Esq MP
	1893/1936	Alban H Gibbs Esq (Later Lord Aldenham)
	1936/1939	The Right Hon Lord Aldenham
	1939/1945	Hon Jasper Ridley
	1945/1949	Lillie, Lady Aldenham
	1951/1954	The Right Hon Lord Ebury
	1955/1976	The Rt Hon Lord Harris, CBE, MC, MA, DL
	1976	The Rt Hon the Earl of Guilford, DL

Chairmen		Prior to 1905 Members took turns at chairing meetings
	1905/1923	Richard Stevens Esq JP
	1924/1929	G J Allen Esq DL, JP
	1929/1940	Col C G Allen, MC
	1940/1956	J C Stevens Esq
	1957/1973	J H Maltby Esq
	1973/1976	R C Chater Esq
	1976/1984	W S Addiscott Esq TD
	1984/1985	A W Adams Esq
	1985 –	Mrs D H E Jeston
Headmasters	*London*	
	1792–1829	Dr Joseph Watson
	1830–1857	T J Watson Esq
	1857–1878	Rev J H Watson BA
	London and Kent	
	1875–1908	Dr R Elliott
	Kent	
	1908–1932	J O White Esq
	1932–1956	A B Swayne Esq OBE
	1956–1976	T Pursglove Esq
	1976 –	B S Armstrong Esq
Secretaries	1792–1804	Rev H Cox Mason
	1804–1806	Rev John Townsend
	1806–1834	Rev Richard Yates, DD, FSA
	1834–1869	Rev William Curling
	1848–1869	Charles Nottidge Esq (Hon Secretary)
	1869–1871	Rev J H Watson, BA, (Headmaster)
	1871–1893	W H Warwick Esq
	1893–1899	W Resbury Few Esq

1899–1928	F H Madden Esq
1928–1933	F W Freeman Esq
1934–1957	Brigadier B L Beddy, DSO
1957–1974	J Coombs Esq
1973 –	D E Downs Esq JP,MBIM